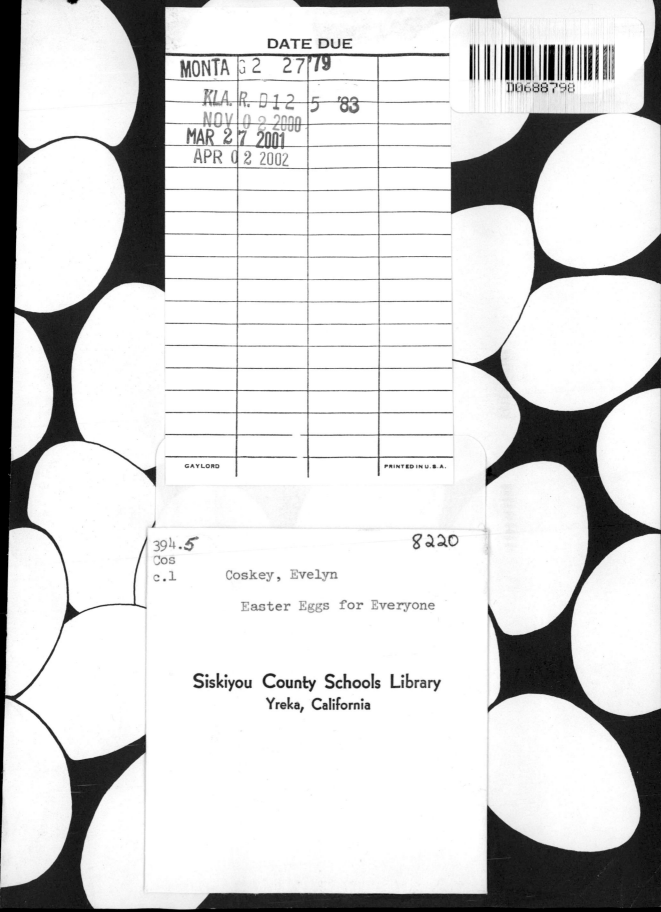

# EASTER EGGS for EVERYONE

# EASTER EGGS FOR EVERYONE

## EVELYN COSKEY

*Drawings by*
GIORGETTA BELL

*Photographs unless otherwise indicated are by*
SID DORRIS

*Nashville* ABINGDON PRESS *New York*

**Library of Congress Cataloging Publication Data**

COSKEY, EVELYN, 1932-
Easter eggs for everyone.
SUMMARY: Discusses the lore and legends of eggs, including Easter eggs, gives instructions for simple and elaborate ways to decorate eggs, and suggests uses for the final product.
Bibliography: p.187
1. Egg decoration. [1. Egg decoration. 2. Handicraft] I. Bell, Giorgetta A., illus. II. Dorris, Sid, illus. III. Title.
TT896.7.C67     745.59'41     72-6680

ISBN 0-687-11492-6

for mary davis fee
and helen post ross

# acknowledgments

I wish to
thank these people
who have helped especially:
Mrs. John Barna for her assistance with the teardrop eggs and
the pin stylus; Mrs. Allen Blumberg for
help in adapting some of the ideas for
use with the special child; Mrs. Betty Law-
rence for help with the peephole eggs; Dr.
Jozef Szczepkowski for information on Polish
Easter eggs; and Roy N. Walters for information on community-wide egg hunts; Mrs. Ina
Thomas supplied information on making an egg
tree for kindergartners; Mrs. Edna Williams and
her kindergarten class demonstrated an egg-
dyeing party for kindergartners.

I also wish to thank *Family Circle Maga-
zine* for permission to adapt for use
their instructions for comic strip
eggs, golden eggs, Tiffany eggs
glace, and the pincushion
styrofoam eggs.

# CONTENTS

# iNTRODuCTiON

Libraries
abound with books
on Christmas handicrafts.
Easter eggs are scarcely men-
tioned. What little information is available is widely scattered, often incomplete
and inaccurate, and all too frequently lo-
cated in obscure, noncirculating sources. It is
almost impossible to find *any* information on
the lovely but less common methods of decorating
Easter eggs, or directions for holding certain types
of Easter entertainments.

This book is the result of a three-year search for these
materials. Every method given has been carefully
tested for accuracy and clarity. All age and ability
groups from pre-schoolers to dedicated artists have
been included. Special information is also given
on adapting some of the techniques to the needs
of the mentally retarded, spastic, and culturally deprived child. The book is intended to
serve as a guide for parents, librarians,
recreation and Scout leaders, and the
general public. Teachers of special
education classes will also
find it of particular
intcrest.

# EGG LORE AND LEGENDS

The egg is one of the oldest symbols known to mankind. Almost from the beginnings of recorded history men have used it to represent the universe. In many cultures, the egg is considered the symbol of the rebirth of the earth out of the bleakness of winter and into the bright promise of spring. The early Indo-Europeans, startled by the sight of a living thing emerging from an apparently dead object, made the egg a fertility symbol, and so it remains to this day. The folklore of almost every nation contains some mention of the egg, and, in many instances, its use is connected with marriage rituals. Today the use of colored eggs at Easter is seldom seen outside those countries in which Christianity is practiced.

In ancient Egypt, one legend tells of the creation of the universe from an enormous egg. Geb, a chief god, whose body is the earth, and Nut, his wife, the sky, produced the egg. From it hatched the bennu bird, or phoenix. The phoenix is said to die by setting fire to its own nest and burning itself to ashes. In the ashes is found an egg from which a new phoenix hatches in time. According to some traditions, the cycle is supposed to be repeated about every fourteen hundred years.

Because of the remarkable way in which the phoenix is reputed to die and come to life again, the bird was accepted by Christianity as a representation of Christ.

15

## Easter Eggs For Everyone

In Hindu mythology one finds the beautiful tale of the world-egg, which was formed in the "waters of chaos" before time and the universe began. The world-egg was made of gold and from it came forth Prajapati, the father of gods, men, and all creatures. Still another version of the same story tells of Prajapati creating the world-egg from his own sweat; the upper half of its shell contained the heavens and the lower section the earth.

Hindu scripture also has a creation story in which the world developed from an egg. After resting for a year, the egg split into several parts. One half of the shell became silver, the other gold. The silver was the earth and the gold the sky. The outer membrane formed the mountains, the inner membrane the clouds and mist, the veins the rivers, and the fluid in the egg the ocean. The sun was born from what was within the egg.

The famous Finnish epic poem, *Kalevala*, tells of the creation of the world from the broken eggs of a teal, a type of duck commonly found on rivers.

The early Hawaiians believed that their largest island was formed by the bursting of an egg laid by a gigantic bird.

The ancient Persian story of creation also centers on the hatching of the world from an enormous egg. The Persians were among the first to make use of colored eggs as gifts at the time of the spring equinox, which marked the beginning of their year.

Although Chinese legends and mythology contain very little mention of eggs, red-dyed eggs were among the traditional offerings made to the god and goddess of the bed, who were considered minor household gods. Their duties consisted of protecting the sleeping chamber and keeping babies from rolling off the hard sleeping platforms.

In other cultures, one finds a great deal of emphasis placed on stories telling about the soul being kept outside of the body and hidden away in an egg.

In one Italian legend, a great cloud which was really a

fairy in disguise, demanded a young girl as tribute from the people of a certain city each year. If the cloud did not get the girl, it threw things at the people and killed them. This went on for a long, long time, and it was not until the king's daughter was sacrificed that anyone became courageous enough to try to stop it. Finally a young man turned himself into an eagle and flew to the fairy palace in the sky. There he found not only the king's daughter but the other girls who had been given to the fairy over the years. He told them to ask the fairy how she could be killed and what would happen to them after she died. They learned that the only way the fairy could die was to have someone kill a tigress with seven heads. In the animal's body was an egg, and if there were any way to hit the fairy in the forehead with that egg, she would die. Otherwise, if the fairy were able to get the egg in her own hands, the tigress would come back to life. By using great imagination and bravery, the young man turned himself into a lion and succeeded in killing the tiger. He took the egg to the fairy and persuaded her to release the captive girls. Then the young man struck the fairy in the forehead with the egg and killed her.

There are many such stories in Russian folklore. One of them tells the tale of Kashtshei, the Deathless, a warlock who carried off a princess and kept her captive in his castle. When a sympathetic prince found her alone one day in the garden, he persuaded her to find out how the warlock could be killed so that they could go off together. After a long struggle and many failures, the princess found that Kashtshei's soul was kept in an egg in a duck in a hare in a basket in a chest on an island in a far-off sea. The prince found the island and got the egg. Then he crushed the egg, killing the warlock at the same time. The prince and princess, apparently, lived happily ever after.

Celtic folklore is another source of these stories. In one tale, a sea beast has carried off the daughter of a king, and

17

an old blacksmith insists that there is only one possible way to kill the beast. In the middle of the lake is an island, and on the island is found Eillid Chasfhion, a white-footed hind. If the hind is caught, a hoodie (a variety of crow) would come out of her body, and if the hoodie is caught, a trout would come from the bird. In the mouth of the trout is an egg, and the soul of the beast is in the egg. So the only way to kill the beast is to get the egg from the trout and break the egg. This is done, and the daughter of the king is rescued.

With the egg assuming so much importance in so many ways, it is not surprising that it played a significant role in festivals marking the beginning of spring. In addition to the early Persians including colored eggs in their springtime observances, the Romans had a similar custom. They believed that the twins, Castor and Pollux, were born from an egg laid by Leda, the swan. Their celebration honoring the twins included races run on egg-shaped tracks and eggs given as prizes and as gifts.

# EASTER EGG CUSTOMS

As Christianity became more widely accepted, the egg assumed even greater importance. It was adopted as the symbol of the new life Christians found in their Savior. Many Christians, especially those who followed the Eastern Orthodox faith, began the practice of giving gifts of eggs on the morning of the Resurrection. The gift expressed a renewal of life through the Resurrection and, for many, also a renewal of faith and love.

In many countries, the eggs were dyed red in remembrance of the blood Christ shed on the cross at Calvary. Ostrich eggs were found in early Christian graves, and in the Middle Ages it was the practice to put a colored egg in a representation of the tomb of Jesus Christ during the Easter liturgy. Some of these eggs were decorated with silver, gold, and jewels. For many people, the egg is also symbolic of the stone rolled away from the Tomb, and it is this representation which appears in egg-rolling contests and other similar Easter observances.

It is not known exactly when or how the custom of coloring eggs at Easter came to Europe, but the practice has been found in an African tribe which was once Christian but later converted to Muhammadanism. One theory is that warriors returning from the Crusades picked up the idea from these people and carried it back to Europe with them. Colored eggs have been a significant part of the Easter celebration since at least the fifteenth century, and there are references to their use as early as the thirteenth.

The Macedonians were the first Christians on record to use eggs in connection with Easter. The children brought all the eggs they could find, dyed them, and sold them in the marketplace. Most of the Macedonian eggs were red, though a few were dyed yellow or green.

In more recent times, the egg has played an important role in both human and agricultural fertility rites. In seventeenth century France, a bride had to break an egg on entering her new home to be certain that she would have children. The Germans and Slavs smeared a mixture of eggs, bread, and flour on their plows on Maundy Thursday to guarantee a rich harvest. On St. George's Day, which is celebrated in early spring and is associated with the beginning of the growing season, the Ukrainians rolled an egg, dyed a solid color and called a *krashanka*, in green oats, then buried it in the ground so that they would be assured of a full harvest unharmed by rain or wind. In Brunswick eggs were begged on Whitsunday, a holiday celebrated on the seventh Sunday after Easter to commemorate the descent of the Holy Spirit on the day of Pentecost. If eggs were refused, the people believed that their hens would not lay.

Some Europeans and Americans in rural areas believed until quite recently that eggs had to be taken from a Guinea nest with a spoon; if human hands touched the nest, the hen would leave it. In the country, it was (and sometimes still is) the custom to place fertile eggs in a hen's nest so that the hen would sit on them and hatch the eggs. If these eggs were put into the nest by a woman, pullets would hatch out, but if they were carried there in a man's hat, cocks would be the result.

The belief that eggs had preventive or healing powers was common. The Ukrainians hung a krashanka on a string and put it around the neck of a seriously ill person to guarantee recovery. If the egg was touched to the part of the body affected by blood poisoning, it was supposed to cure the disease.

The Pennsylvania Dutch put a great deal of value on eggs laid on Good Friday. These eggs were used to prevent sore mouth in a baby, to cure goiter, and to be sure of getting speckled chicks. Good Friday eggs, if they were handled properly, could also keep a house from being struck by lightning.

It is interesting to note that eggs play almost no part in the Easter celebrations of Mexico and South America. Nor do the American Indians place much emphasis on Easter eggs.

Easter eggs also have scant importance in Spain. However, there is an Asturian village called Pola de Siero in which there is an annual contest to see who can produce the most beautiful Easter egg. The eggs are elaborately painted, and the competition is keen.

On Good Friday, in Catalonia, in Spain, dessert is *mona*, a large bun. For children too young to receive First Communion, these buns are decorated with eggs, one for each year of the child's life. The eggs are often colored and painted, and each child is expected to go to the pastry shop to pick up his own *mona*. After the child has made his First Communion, the practice is immediately stopped, and he goes on to more adult observances. The same custom is followed in the Balearic Islands, also a part of Spain.

In England eggs have long played an important role in the Easter celebration. At the time of King Edward I, who died in 1307, the use of decorated eggs was an Easter custom in the royal household. These eggs were either stained or covered with gold leaf. Later, Pope Paul V provided a ritual for consecrating Easter eggs in England, Scotland, and Ireland. When the Church of England became Protestant in the sixteenth century, the ritual was dropped along with a number of other practices belonging to the Roman Catholic faith. (Probably for this reason, egg-decorating was never of great importance in the early American colonies because the majority of the settlers were Protestant.)

In spite of its origin, egg-decorating continued to be popular in England. In the early 1800s, scratch-carving was one of the favorite ways of decorating Easter eggs. The egg was dyed a solid color, and then a design, often very elaborate and frequently bearing the recipient's name and birth date, was scratched out on the shell with a needle or other sharp tool. Sometimes these eggs were used to establish the owner's official birth date if this information was needed for legal purposes.

Scratch-carving was also very popular in the Pennsylvania Dutch and Moravian sections of the United States in the late eighteenth century. The American scratch-carved eggs featured certain motifs: tulips, flat hearts, and birds. Whether of British or American origin, these early scratch-carved eggs are regarded as collectors' items today.

Calico eggs were also very popular in America during that period. In those days, fabrics were not at all colorfast, and people expected them to lose color when they were washed. So women took eggs—never ones to be eaten because the dye was poisonous—and wrapped them in scraps of brightly colored, printed cloth. The eggs were boiled in their tied-on cloth dresses. When the eggs were unwrapped, they were decorated with the patterns from the cloth.

English children of today go about begging for eggs at Easter. This is called "pace-egging" from the old word for Easter, *Pasch*. In the northern part of England, the eggs are saved throughout Holy Week for use in egg-rolling contests which are held on Easter Day.

Scottish children paint hardcooked eggs and roll them down grassy slopes on Easter morning. Most do not stop to remember that they are doing this to commemorate the rolling away of the stone from in front of Christ's tomb. In Scotland some children also play ball on Easter, but they use dyed eggs instead of a regular ball.

## Easter Egg Customs

Easter eggs are particularly important in Ireland. In many areas of the country, children build little nests from stones. They do this on Palm Sunday. During Holy Week, the children collect all the duck and goose eggs they can find and hide them away in the nests. On Easter Sunday the eggs are given as gifts, shared with children too young to have their own nests—and eaten!

Irish adults also give Easter eggs as gifts. The number is determined by an ancient saying which is known in several versions among country folk:

> *"One egg for true gentleman,*
> *Two for gentlemen,*
> *Three for churl,*
> *Four for lowest churl."*

The German people have many Easter Egg customs. It is so common for German children to receive eggs as Easter gifts that the eggs are known as "owed eggs."

For a long time, it was a German custom for people to give each other three dyed eggs accompanied by a poem as an Easter gift. Some still do. This is the poem they use, translated into English:

> *All good things are three.*
> *Therefore I present you three Easter eggs;*
> *Faith and Hope and Love.*
> *Never lose from your heart*
> *Faith to the church, hope in God,*
> *And love Him to thy death.*[1]

For several weeks before Easter, German housewives blow all the eggs they use in cooking. To blow an egg, a small hole

---

[1] Grace E. Storms, *The Family Celebrates Easter* (Boston: Pilgrim Press, 1954), p. 10.

is made in each end of the egg, and the contents are blown out through one of the holes. The empty shells are rinsed out and saved for use in a variety of Easter games or are decorated to make ornaments for the Easter egg tree.

Easter egg trees have long been part of the folk life of Germany and Switzerland. Like so many customs now observed at Easter, the first egg trees had nothing at all to do with the Resurrection. They were decorated in honor of the of the arrival of spring and were made by impaling uncolored eggshells of various kinds on twiggy bushes growing out of doors. Though egg trees like these are sometimes seen today, the modern ones more closely resemble a Christmas tree than they do their own ancestors.

In the 1890s very elaborate Easter egg trees were popular in Germany. Commonly made from evergreen trees which were placed on a table in the living room, they were trimmed with blown, dyed eggs which were often filled with candy. A loop of contrasting ribbon was glued to the broad end of the egg and served as a hanger. Sugar figures, tinsel ornaments, and cake animals (especially rabbits and lambs) were also favorite decorations for the egg tree. Underneath, the Easter Rabbit, and sometimes the Paschal Lamb for company, presided over a nest of gifts. Except for the absence of snow, there was not a great deal of difference between a German Christmas tree of the period and an Easter egg tree.

Then, as now, Germany produced many of the greeting cards sold in America. Naturally, Easter egg trees appeared on a number of these cards. By the early 1900s, the custom had spread to the United States and was especially popular in areas where there were many people of German background. Even today, though egg trees are common, they are more frequently seen in the Pennsylvania Dutch country than in other places.

In Austria Easter eggs are frequently decorated by covering them with tiny leaves or flowers, then binding the leaves in place with very fine thread or covering the egg with gauze. The egg is dyed, and a white design appears on the colored background.

In the Tyrol, a mountainous district, which is partly in Austria and partly in Italy, children spend Easter Eve traveling from farm to farm, carrying baskets and torches. As they walk they sing, and at each farmhouse the children beg for eggs. The farmers' wives compete with each other to see who can give the children the prettiest eggs.

In the Eastern part of the Netherlands, many of the customs are of Saxon origin. The people sometimes call it *Sassy*. Years ago, Dutch people living in this area made Sassy-type Easter eggs by placing a square of cloth on the table and covering it with a layer of onion skins. Next, they put a layer of tiny flowers and leaves over the onion skins and placed an egg in the middle. The whole thing was wrapped around the egg and the bundle tied with string. Then the bundle was put into a kettle and boiled for about twenty minutes in water which contained coffee grounds. The results were something like the Austrian eggs. Dutch children sometimes decorate eggs in the old Sassy way even today.

Belgian children make nests of hay and hide them in the grass on Easter Eve. They know that the Easter Bunny will fill the nests with dyed and chocolate eggs on Easter morning.

When the church bells are silenced after mass on Holy Thursday, Roman Catholic children in France and Italy are told that the bells have gone to Rome to bring back the Easter eggs. Holy Thursday, or Maundy Thursday as it is known in Protestant churches, is the Thursday before Easter and is a time of special observances in most Christian churches.

In France, children who make their first confessions on Holy Saturday sometimes take gifts of eggs to the priest.

In Eastern Europe, especially in Poland, Russia, and the Ukraine, parts of the Easter meal are taken to church to be blessed by the priest on Holy Saturday. The long Lenten fast, which sometimes includes abstinence from eating eggs, ends after mass on Easter morning and the oldest member of each family divides a blessed egg into as many pieces as there are people present at the meal and shares it with them.

In Polish villages, *dyngus* (in some areas, *smigus*) is practiced on Easter Monday, which is a holiday. Young men douse the girls with water as a way of wishing them good looks and health. In return, the girls give each young man an Easter egg. These eggs are usually decorated in the manner of the region. Among upper and middle class Poles, cologne is used instead of water and candy replaces the decorated egg.

Easter eggs have always had particular religious significance in Russia, and even today those who are practicing members of the Eastern Orthodox faith decorate their eggs in the old manner and take them to church to be blessed by the priest on Easter Eve. Many Russian Easter eggs are dyed red and decorated with the letters XV, the initial letters of the words, *Khrystos voskres*, meaning "Christ is risen." Among these people it is the practice to exchange red eggs with one's friends, greeting them with "Christ is risen!" The friend replies *vo istine voskres* "He is risen indeed!" This custom is also followed in other countries where the Eastern Orthodox faith is of major importance.

Russia is well known for the great beauty of her Easter eggs, but many of these do not originate with the hen. In *My St. Petersburg*, Martha E. Almedingen tells of the importance of the Easter eggs at the *Verba*, a fair which lasted from Palm Sunday through Holy Week. The Verba was named for the pussy willows which are used in Russia instead of palms to decorate churches and homes during the sacred time. When Miss Almedingen was a girl in 1908, some of the most interesting booths at the Verba were those which sold Easter eggs. Farmers' wives came in from the region around the Baltic to sell eggs in round baskets lined with green and gray moss, and they trimmed their wares with chicks

26

made from fluffs of yellow wool. These eggs were considered so common that few people prized them. There were other eggs more worthy of attention. The white china eggs with views of the city of St. Petersburg painted on them were fascinating—and expensive. There were also eggs made from clear glass and containing panoramas of the Resurrection inside. Other exciting Easter eggs were made of gloriously perfumed soap tinted in delicate colors. Still others were made from jasper, malachite, and other precious or semi-precious materials. Most of these eggs, of course, were small and many of them were sold individually, resting on beds of black velvet.

Of all Russian Easter eggs, perhaps few are more famous than the Fabergé eggs. These eggs, indirectly, had their beginning because the Russians traditionally make gifts of eggs at Easter. These are not ordinary gifts but have deep symbolic meaning: They stand for a renewal of faith in personal relationships and imply a great deal of love.

After the murder of Tsar Alexander II in 1881, the tsarina, Maria Fydoronva, became very ill and depressed. To divert her from her shock and grief, Tsar Alexander III asked Karl Fabergé, a jeweler, to make an Easter egg as a surprise for the tsarina. Fabergé was famous for the quality and originality of his work. The egg was to be kept a complete secret until Easter morning, when it was given to the delighted tsarina. Later, Tsar Nicholas II, determined to follow his father's example, commissioned Fabergé to make an egg each Easter for his mother and his wife. Like the first Fabergé egg, all were kept closely guarded secrets until Easter morning. Each one was a masterpiece. Every egg was elaborately jeweled and many had intricate surprises inside. Fabergé made more than fifty of these eggs for the Rusian royal family. During and after the Russian Revolution, most of them were taken out of the country, and many have found their way into museums and private collections. A considerable number of the Fabergé eggs are now in America.

27

# Easter Eggs For Everyone

In Hungary boys sprinkle their girl friends with perfumed water and are rewarded with a meal of hot bread, wine, and Easter eggs.

Ukrainian girls make their cheeks rosy by rubbing them with red-dyed *krashanky*, solid-colored hardcooked eggs. At Easter, the Ukrainians and other Slavic people like to decorate eggs in mosiac-like patterns. These intricate eggs are called *pysanky*. There are so many things to tell about pysanky that a whole chapter is devoted to them.

Very little attention is paid to Easter eggs in the Scandinavian countries. Many families paint or color eggs, but the customs belong to the individual families, not to the countries.

Armenian Christian families traditionally eat a meal of red-dyed eggs, roast lamb, and a special bread on Easter. After the family has eaten, the boys play games with the remaining red eggs. Armenian children are given Easter gifts of blown eggs decorated with pictures of the Risen Christ, the Virgin Mary, and other religious themes.

Children who live in Iraq, a country near Turkey, gather all the eggs they can during Lent and sell them in the marketplace for Easter.

In the United States, children have a wide variety of Easter customs. Children of Urkainian descent are likely to be taught the art of decorating pysanky, and almost all like to decorate Easter eggs in some way. Many American children take part in Easter egg rolling.

Easter egg rolling is a very old and popular sport. In many Christian countries, Easter Monday is a national holiday, and the festivities almost always include egg rolling. Though the rules vary somewhat from place to place, egg rolling is usually done on a hillside. The children—and often adults, too— roll their eggs down the hill. The egg rolling the longest distance without cracking wins. In some parts of Holland the winner receives a prize of 101 eggs.

In the United States, an egg rolling is held each Easter

Monday on the south lawn of the White House in Washington, D.C. Only children under the age of twelve and the adults who accompany them are admitted to the White House grounds. The children bring their own eggs and make up their own egg games. Bands from the armed forces provide entertainment for the guests.

Easter egg rolling has been a popular holiday activity in Washington ever since Abraham Lincoln was president. There might have been egg rollings there before that, but there is no definite record. At first the annual event took place on Capitol Hill. During the time when Rutherford B. Hayes was president, Congress banned egg rolling there, and it was moved to the south lawn of the White House. When World War II broke out in 1941, egg rolling was discontinued, but it was resumed in 1953 on orders from Pres. Dwight D. Eisenhower. The event has been held every year since then.

There is also an egg rolling held each year in New York City's Central Park. Other cities in the United States hold similar events, but these are the best known.

Easter egg trees are very popular in the United States. Many school children make them to decorate their classrooms, and often communities have large outdoor trees. Though egg trees are seen in many parts of America, the greatest number are made in the Pennsylvania Dutch Country.

# EASTER EGGS TODAY

Though dyed eggs were seldom associated with Easter before the thirteenth century, the story is very different today. In many parts of the Christian world, the egg is a vital part of the Easter celebration. Not only do small children derive pleasure from coloring eggs, but Easter eggs have become big business.

In the beginning, all dyes were made from things found in nature. If a red dye was wanted, logwood or carrots or dried cochineal insects were used; for yellow, furze flowers or onion skins or an ear of dried corn; for green, boiled hay or alder bark did nicely. Today, in almost all parts of the world, one simply goes into a store, buys a packet of inexpensive, easily used, usually edible egg coloring, and goes home to spend a pleasant hour or two coloring eggs. The process used to take days, sometimes weeks if one lived in the Ukraine and decorated pysanky. The production and sale of egg-decorating products now occupies all the time of a number of large companies and many other smaller firms spend part of their efforts in these things. Even the once home-made pysanky equipment can now be bought, and a kit containing all the necessary materials is available on a mail order basis.

On a smaller scale, many people have discovered that the making and sale of the more elaborate types of Easter eggs provides an excellent source of extra income for groups or individuals. Well-made and reasonably priced, there is considerable demand for these items at bazaars, on special order, or through handicraft shops. Those lacking the time or skill for the more intricate techniques should have little difficulty finding someone to do the work for them, for a price. In both the United States and Canada, clever women of Ukrainian descent long ago learned the market value of their pysanky-making skills.

In some areas, handicrafts shops hold egg-decorating contests with the winner receiving as a prize some item sold in the shop. These contests are usually divided into age and ability groups. They provide an exciting creative outlet, and good publicity for the shop sponsoring the contest.

As a craft activity, egg-decorating is one of the most satisfying things anyone can do. There is literally no age or ability group which cannot find something to enjoy and do well in the art. A small child, under supervision, can dye a hard-cooked egg a bright, solid color; an older child may use it to meet a craft requirement in Scouts or some other group; the somewhat bored teen-ager will be challenged by tie-dyed eggs (page 59) or Lieutenant Flap (page 119); an artistically inclined housewife, feeling trapped in the suburbs, might get just the lift she needs by trying peephole eggs (page 134) or experimenting with pysanky (pages 85-92). An older person, perhaps confined to a rest home, will find egg heads (pages 110-22) interesting without being too tiring.

## EASTER EGGS AND THE SPECIAL CHILD

Even the quite seriously handicapped need not be deprived of the fun of decorating eggs. All but a few of the techniques described in this book can be done by most of the mentally retarded, and many of the more severely retarded can have fun making rainbow eggs (page 60).

Since the retarded usually lack fine finger control, they should not attempt to make a pin stylus. There is too much possibility of driving the pin into themselves instead of into the stick. For the higher levels of skill, when a technique requiring the use of a pin stylus seems appropriate, have the stylus ready beforehand.

The use of plastic eggs is often wise when working with children or others with impaired finger control or any tentency towards spasticity. The eggs may be purchased at low cost and are frequently found in variety or hobby supply shops. These eggs may be used with almost any method not requiring the use of dye. All-purpose white glue successfully holds decorations in place on plastic eggs.

Even blind children will find that they can manage some of the techniques which require more emphasis on a sense of touch than on color discrimination, for example, the Polish *binesgraas eggs* (page 94), the golden eggs (page 98), or some of the egg heads and animals (pages 110-30).

Though all children living in a rural setting may like to combine a nature walk to gather materials for natural dyes with their egg-decorating project, this is an especially good activity for the culturally deprived. Along with the intended collection of egg-decorating materials, the clever instructor can point out many of the things seen by others but usually missed by these less fortunate children.


Easter egg decorating, as an art and as a craft, goes back many centuries, but it is as current as the latest moon exploration. It is one of the least limited craft activities; no matter how poor a home may be, it would be hard to find one in which there is *nothing* to use for egg-decorating. A tiny child can have fund doing it—or an elderly grandparent. Have fun. Egg-decorating is for *you*.

# GENERAL EQUIPMENT, TECHNIQUES, AND MATERIALS

Most things needed for egg decoration are commonly found in the home, and those that are not may usually be ought at the supermarket or hobby shop. There are few exceptions.

## WHAT KIND OF EGG?

Unless dyed eggs are to be kept under refrigeration until they are eaten, it is wise to regard them as an investment in fun, rather than food. Cooked eggs spoil rapidly if they are not kept cold. Under normal conditions, hardcooked eggs remain good to eat for three or four days at room temperature or for up to ten days if refrigerated.

*CAUTION*

Eggs for dyeing should be clean, white, and free of grease; grease keeps the dye from adhering to the egg. If you plan to blow the eggs and use the contents in cooking, freshness is more important than it is if the eggs are to be hardcooked for dyeing. Especially for use with children, small-sized grade B eggs may be an economy. They provide just as much fun without the high cost often associated with prime eggs. White eggs from other kinds of poultry may be used, if you live in an area where they are available. For some of the more elaborate cutout or jeweled eggs, large duck eggs are sometimes easier to work with.

Unless you get your eggs from a farm it is good to remember that most egg companies spray store-bound eggs with a protective coating of mineral oil before marketing them. This replaces the bloom, or natural coating, which is washed off during the processing. The spray seals off the pores of the egg and prolongs freshness on the shelf. Unfortunately, it also produces a slick, nonporous shell, which takes dye much less well than an untreated eggshell.

Ocasionally you will find an egg which refuses to accept dye. If at all possible, substitute another egg.

## EQUIPMENT FOR DYEING EGGS

*Egg holder*

*Cups.* Use one cup for each color of egg dye. The cup should be large enough to allow the dye to cover the egg completely and provide sufficient room to move the egg in the dye bath without splashing dye on the table. Ordinary kitchen cups do very well. Disposable hot drink cups also work well. The foam cups are especially good. Do not use disposable cups intended for cold drinks unless you are using cold water dye. These cups usually have a waxy finish which will dissolve when it comes into contact with hot liquids. The dissolved wax will spoil the egg dye.

*Egg holders.* Egg holders come with most commercially sold egg-dye kits. They are made from thin, stiff wire and have a loop at one end large enough to support an egg while it is being dyed. There is a handle on the other end. If you do not have a wire egg holder, use a tablespoon instead.

34

## OTHER ITEMS FOR EGG-DECORATING

*Crayons.* Most of the time, when the directions call for crayons, you may use any wax crayon. However, if the directions call for Crayolas, do not substitute wax crayons. The result will not be the same.

*White wax crayons.* These clear wax crayons are included in many commercial egg-dye kits. Sometimes they are called magic pencils or magic crayons, because they make marks on the egg which are invisible until the egg is dyed. Then the marks appear white against the colored surface of the egg. Or, you may dye the egg a light color first, then mark on it with the white wax crayon. Dip the marked egg into a darker dye, which can be used successfully over the first color. You will have light colored marks against a darker background. These crayons are made from uncolored paraffin. If you do not have one, you may substitute the white crayon found in many crayon sets. The results will not be exactly the same because these crayons have been colored white and will make an opaque white mark on the egg.

*Cotton cloth*. When the directions call for cotton cloth, use 6-inch squares of white or colorfast, cotton material. The cloth should be free from any traces of starch or sizing. Scraps from a discarded bedsheet are good. Do not substitute synthetic fabrics or partly-synthetic materials. These fibers do not always take the dye in the same way as cotton does and may not produce the result you would get with cotton.

*Felt-tipped pens*. Felt-tipped pens are used in a number of egg-decorating methods. They are especially useful for marking the features on egg heads or egg animals. If you use them for this purpose, be sure to use pens with fine points. Be careful about using felt-tipped pens with cooked eggs. The dye often bleeds through the eggshell and will affect the cooked egg inside. *Never eat an egg which has been damaged by this dye*

CAUTION

*Water color paints*. Watercolors produce a -transparent finish on the eggshells. They are very good for decorating Easter eggs, and small children like to use them.

*Tempera or poster paints*. These paints make an opaque finish on eggshells. They are especially good for use with brown eggs, since the color of the eggshell does not show through the paint. You may buy these paints in either prepared or powdered form. If you use the powdered paints, mix the powder with water until the paint is about the consistency of heavy cream.

*Brushes.* For most egg-decorating purposes water color brushes of the quality found in variety stores do very well. Get at least two brushes: One should be fine-pointed for doing small details and the other medium-sized for average work. Adults and older children who are doing more detailed work with watercolors will get better results with higher quality brushes, which are available in art supply stores.

*Pencils.* A lead pencil is sometimes used in egg decorating to make guide lines. The marks should be just dark enough to be seen. Pencil marks on an egg cannot be removed without very noticeable smudging. A hard (number 3) pencil is most satisfactory.

*Rubber bands.* These elastic bands have two purposes in egg-decorating. First, they serve as guides for dividing the egg into sections in decorating certain types, such as golden eggs or pysanky. A medium-sized rubber band usually does very well. When used as a guide, the width of the band is not important. Second, rubber bands are sometimes used to keep egg dye away from certain parts of the egg while it is being dyed. This is done in striped eggs and in plaid eggs. When the rubber band is used in this way, or to mark off a border in some types of pysanky, a wide band should be used. In either case, the rubber band should fit snugly around the egg, lengthwise or cross-wise.

*Masking Tape.* Narrow widths of masking tape may be used in the same way as rubber bands; as guides for marking the egg or as protection of certain spots from the dye. Tape is easy to handle and makes very sharp, clear stripes.

*All-purpose white glue.* This useful glue is sold in almost any supermarket or variety store. There are both waterproof and washable types. Either one may be used in egg-decorating, but the washable kind is best for use with children.

*Household cement.* Clear, all-purpose household cement is usually sold in tubes. It is found in most variety stores and in many hobby shops. This glue dries very rapidly and is especially useful in making cutout eggs, jeweled eggs, and for gluing bases on stand-up eggs. It is difficult to remove glue from surfaces where it might be dropped, so work on a well-covered table if you are using it. A wooden toothpick is very useful for applying household cement. This *CAUTION* glue should be used only in a well-ventilated place.

*White paste.* School or library paste is used in a variety of ways in egg-decorating. It may usually be substituted for all-purpose white glue, and should be substituted for it with small children. If you do not have white paste on hand, you may use a small amount of wallpaper paste, or make your own flour and water paste.

*Rubber cement.* Rubber cement is sometimes used in egg-decorating because it stays sticky for a few minutes before it dries. It is often used with *binsegraas* eggs and *binsegraas* modern style and may be used with other types of eggs. Rubber cement is usually sold in small jars or cans and may be bought in stationery and art supply stores. It is quite inexpensive. Rubber cement is easy to remove from the skin and from most surfaces if it is spilled. If you are using rubber cement, do work on a paper-covered table.

*Darning needle.* A darning needle is useful for puncturing the ends and inner membrane of an egg before blowing it. It may also be used to etch out a design on a scratch-carved egg. Use the type of needle which has a sharp point, and be sure it is absolutely clean before you use it if you are blowing eggs.

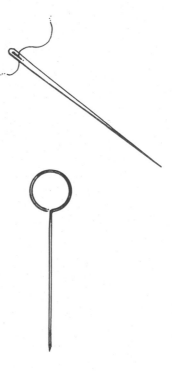

*Skewer.* A metal skewer may be used instead of a darning needle when preparing eggs for blowing. Be sure it is very clean before you use it.

*Knitting needle.* If you are going to paint an eggshell with tempera paint, you may find it easier to handle if you run a thin knitting needle through both blowing holes in the egg, using the needle to hold the eggshell as you paint it.

*Ice pick.* A clean, sharp-pointed ice pick may be used to prepare eggs for blowing. Be sure to keep darning needles, skewers, and ice picks away from small children.

*CAUTION*

*Manicure scissors.* Sharp-pointed manicure scissors are used to cut away the excess eggshell in cut-out eggs and for similar purposes. The type with slightly curved blades do best. Do not use your best manicure scissors in working with eggs. You will ruin them.

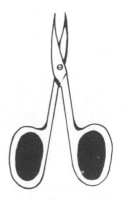

*Scissors.* Except for the few instances in which manicure scissors are needed, ordinary household or school scissors are used in egg-decorating. The blunt-pointed type are best for small children.

*Tweezers.* Tweezers are very useful in handling small things—beads, sequins, the smaller figures in peephole eggs, etc. A pair from the variety store works well.

*Curtain rings.* Small plastic or metal curtain rings may be glued to the bottom of any decorated egg which you want to preserve as an ornament. The ring will make a base and the egg will stand up.

*Miniature figures.* Small figures are used in cut-out eggs and in peephole eggs. They are often found in hobby and specialty shops, but you may have to hunt around a bit before you find what you want. Greeting cards offer a good supply of figures to be cut out and used.

*Beads, sequins, narrow gilt braid, etc.* Your jewelry box may be a good source of small beads. All these items may be found in hobby shops, in stores that carry fabrics and sewing supplies, and in some variety stores.

*Tiny flowers.* These are used in cutout and peephole eggs. The flowers are usually made of plastic or felt and may be found in many variety stores or hobby shops.

*Narrow ribbon.* Ribbon is used in some types of collage eggs and is often used to make hangers for eggs used to decorate an egg tree. Sometimes the family scrap box will provide what you need. If not, the variety store or sewing center should have it.

*Stylus.* A stylus is used to apply melted beeswax to the surface of the egg when making batik-type Easter eggs such as pysanky. There are two types of stylus.

A pin stylus is a very simple stylus made by pushing the point of a common straight pin into the end of a wooden skewer or the end of a pencil. The pin should go far enough into the shaft that it will stay in place when the stylus is being used. The wax is applied with the head of the pin. A pin stylus is an excellent tool for a beginner to use.

A pysanky stylus consists of a brass head attached to a wooden shaft. You may make your own stylus by following the directions on page 79, or you may purchase one. Commercially made pysanky styluses come with fine, medium, or heavy points, and an adequate one is very modestly priced.

*Beeswax.* This wax is used to mark the designs on batik-type eggs such as pysanky. It is used because it has a high melting point, better covering ability, and greater resistance to dyes. Beeswax candles are expensive to buy, but you might be able to get used ones from a church. The easiest and least expensive way to get beeswax is to buy it in block form where sewing supplies are sold. Often sewing thread is strengthened by rubbing it over the beeswax before using it. One block should cost less than a dollar, and will go a long way.

*Candles.* The flame of ordinary paraffin candles is used to heat the stylus when making batik-process eggs.

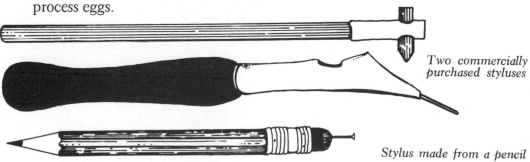

*Two commercially purchased styluses*

*Stylus made from a pencil*

41

## HOW TO HARDCOOK AN EGG

If you plan to hardcook your eggs for coloring and eating, it is important to know the correct way to do it. An improperly cooked egg is likely to have a cracked shell or to be rubbery in texture when it is eaten. The most efficient way to hardcook an egg is actually the easiest.

Begin with clean, white eggs, fresh from the farm if you can possibly get them. Have the eggs at room temperature to keep the shells from cracking as they cook. Put the eggs in a clean, grease-free enamel, steel, or glass pan, which is

*CAUTION*    large enough to hold them without crowding. (Do not use an aluminum pan for hardcooking eggs. A harmless chemical reaction between the pan and the eggshells will keep the dye from adhering properly.) Completely cover the eggs with cold water, adding enough extra water to come one inch over the top of the eggs. Heat until the water boils, and immediately remove the pan from the stove. Cover and allow it to stand off the heat for 25 minutes. Rinse the eggs with cold water. This makes the eggs easier to handle, and will make it simpler to remove the shells later on. It does not matter about the temperature of the eggs when you are coloring them solid colors or using many other decorating techniques, but eggs at room temperature are much easier to handle than very hot ones.

42

# HOW TO BLOW AN EGG

Blown eggs are used in many ways. Eggs for use on an Easter egg tree must be blown, and any egg to be dyed may be. If the eggs are to be kept as ornaments, they will be more satisfactory if they are blown before you dye them.

## Materials

> Clean, fresh eggs, most often white—uncooked, of
> course
> Darning needle or an ice pick—very clean
> Bowl
> Drinking straw, if desired

## Method

1-Using the darning needle or ice pick, make a small hole in one end of the egg and a slightly larger one in the other end. Be sure to pierce the inner membrane at both ends. The egg will blow out more easily if you also puncture the yolk. See pictures, page 44.
2-Hold the egg over the bowl. Place your mouth over the small hole and blow with firm and steady force. The contents of the egg will come out the larger hole. Or, if you prefer, hold the end of a drinking straw firmly against the smaller hole and blow into that.
3-Rinse the egg out well with water, and allow it to air-dry before using it.

## Another Method

1-If you are planning to make confetti eggs or use the blown eggshell in a similar way, instead of making a small

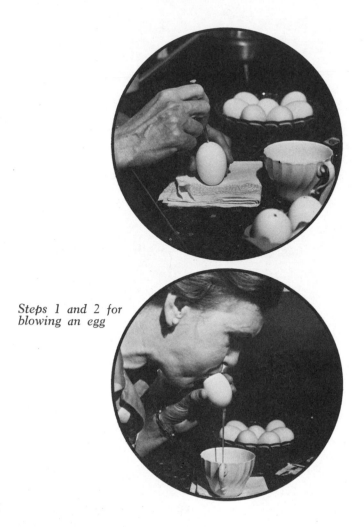

*Steps 1 and 2 for blowing an egg*

hole in each end of the egg, just make one hole about the size of a dime in one end of the egg.

2-Shake out the contents of the egg. Place a piece of tape over the hole.

Children who are not feeling well should not assist in egg-blowing. It is important to remove any lipstick or other grease-based lip makeup before blowing an egg.

The contents of the eggs may be used in cooking for any dish which does not require the separation of egg whites and egg yolks.

# EASTER EGGS WITH dye

## COLORS

In many types of Easter eggs, one color is dyed over a previous color to get a third, pleasing color. Or, you may want to mix two or more colors to get a color you do not have. Some colors may be successfully combined, but others may not be mixed. Red, yellow, and blue are called primary colors. By mixing them in the right combinations and amounts, you can get any color you want. If you are coloring eggs with dye, be sure to start with the lightest color in the combination. These colors may be combined:

Yellow plus blue (equal amounts) makes green.
Yellow plus red (use more red) makes orange.
Red plus blue (use more red) makes purple.

If you want a pastel color, use smaller amounts of each color in proportion to the amount of water used. If you want a darker shade, use more dye in proportion to the amount of water. Do not change the amount of water called for in the individual dyeing processes.

If you are working with tempera or poster paints, make pastel colors by adding white to the paint. Make deeper tones by adding black to the paint, a very little at a time.

45

## NATURAL DYES

Until the second half of the nineteenth century, virtually all egg dyeing was done with natural dyes. Even after commercially produced colors for eggs came on the market, many people hesitated to use them for fear that child would be poisoned if an egg cracked during cooking and some of the dye got inside the shell. Today few Americans bother with natural dyes, though they are still quite widely used in some parts of Europe. Natural dyes will produce very soft shades not found in commercial egg dyes. Some of the ingredients for natural dyes may even be found in cities. Though working with them can be quite messy, it is often fun to use natural egg dyes for a change.

Do not gather plants for natural dyes in state or national

# Easter Eggs with Dye

parks or forests. Plants in these places are often protected by law. Even where they are not, they should be left for others to enjoy. Regardless of where you gather your plants, never gather any that are in very small supply; if you do, you may be helping to make the species extinct.

Since some natural dyes are not edible, use only blown eggs when experimenting with them—unless you are absolutely sure the dye is safe for food. CAUTION

## Materials

Bark, leaves, or flowers. See the list beginning on page 48 to see which part of each type of plant you will use to make dye from it.

Large enamel pot or kettle

Large strainer or collander

Cloth to line the strainer or collander (A piece of worn out bedsheet is ideal. Or use cheesecloth.)

Medium-sized bowl

China or glass cups for each color of dye.

Vinegar. Use 1 tablespoon for each cup of dye.
   Do not use vinegar with onion-skin dye. CAUTION

## Method

1-Carefully go over the material you plan to use, removing all dirt and bits of debris. Wash the material in plenty of cold water.

2-Chop leaves or flowers fine. Break bark into small bits. The amount of material you use will determine the depth of color in the finished dye.

3-Put the dye material in the pot or kettle. Add enough water to cover it completely.

4-Boil gently for at least five minutes. The exact length of time will be determined by the material you are using and by the depth of color you want.

5-Strain the dye through the cloth in the strainer or collander into the bowl. Pour some of the dye into a cup.

6-Add one tablespoon of vinegar to each dup of dye dye solution. Do not add vinegar to dye made from boiled onion skins because it will affect the color.

7-Spoon the dye over the egg until it is the shade you want.

These things make good natural dyes. Most of them may be found quite easily in the country, and some can be obtained in the city. In the city, there are a variety of sources: the grocery store (try a store specializing in Spanish foods for saffron), a vacant lot, your mother's pantry, or sometimes (always with permission from the director) in a park.

*Yellow*    Onion skins—safe for use with hardcooked
            eggs
       Goldenrod stems, leaves, and flowers
       Pear leaves
       Roots of staghorn sumac
       Celandine
       Tanglewood stems
       Apple bark
       Saffron (5 or 6 pieces)
       Alder catkins
       Hickory bark

**Red**    Red onion skins—safe for use with hardcooked eggs

Bloodroot (only if very plentiful in your area and not protected by conservation laws)

Juice from fresh beets—safe for use with hardcooked eggs. Do not use the juice from canned beets because this is mainly water. It does not produce enough color for use on eggshells.

Madder root

Logwood

**Green**    Birch leaves

Spanish onion skins—the outer coating—safe for food

Elderberry leaves

Rhubarb leaves

Moss

**Pink**    Sassafras roots

**Brown**    Bark of shining sumac

Walnut hulls, well aged (Use rubber gloves when working with walnut hulls. They stain very badly.)

## CREPE PAPER EGG DYE

If you cannot find the color of dye you need, and if you are working with blown eggs, satisfactory dye can be made from crepe paper. Since this method is very messy, it should be used only as a last resort. If you have a pair of rubber gloves, wear them when making this dye.

Never use crepe paper dye with eggs which will be used for food.

*CAUTION*

### Materials

Crepe paper—a piece about 20 inches by 20 inches for each color

Medium-sized bowl

¾ cup warm water

### Method

1-Cut up the crepe paper and put the pieces in the bowl. You do not need to make the pieces very small.

2-Pour the warm water over the paper and let it soak for at least two minutes, or, until most of the color is out of the paper.

3-Squeeze the moisture out of the paper and discard. Use the colored water for egg dye.

## SOLID COLORS

When most people think of coloring eggs, they think of solid colors. Eggs dyed solid colors are also the basis of many other decorating techniques.

Allow a cup or glass for each color egg dye you plan to use and be sure to have vinegar on hand. Most commercially packaged egg colors require the use of vinegar to set the color so that it will not rub off the egg easily. If your egg-coloring kit does not include an egg holder (a wire handle with a loop on one end large enough to support an egg) have a tablespoon handy for each color. You will need something to use for dipping the egg in and out of the dye bath, and either the egg holder or tablespoon will do very well.

Follow the directions on packaged egg coloring for the exact temperature of the water and the amount of vinegar to be used. There is a great deal of difference among commercially sold egg colors, and what is right with one of them is completely wrong with another. You may also use food coloring, liquid or paste, for eggs. Again, following the directions given on the package.

Use the egg holder or tablespoon to dip the egg in and out of the dye bath. Do this until the egg is the shade you want. Or, leave the egg in the coloring, completely covered with it, until the egg is the desired shade. If you want to dye eggs intense shades of solid colors, double the amount of dye to each cup.

If you are coloring blown eggs, you will need to keep turning them and forcing them under the dye bath so that they will take the color evenly. When the inside of the egg becomes filled with the dye, it will remain immersed. This is especially important to remember when dyeing blown eggs

very dark colors. Sometimes eggs must remain in these colors overnight to get the proper depth of color.

Before handling them, allow the colored eggs to dry on paper toweling, in the egg holder, or in a drying rack which comes with some egg-coloring kits.

If you get an egg which seems to resist the color, try adding additional vinegar to the dye bath. This will help cut through the coating of oil sprayed on commercially sold eggs, and the dye should take better. Once in a long while you will find an egg which refuses to accept coloring. If possible, substitute another egg and decorate the resistant egg with some other method which does not call for the use of dye.

If you have an egg which is marred by fingerprints, sponge it with alcohol before dyeing.

## SIMPLE DECORATIONS

There is almost no end to the ways in which eggs may be decorated. For use with "small people," some of these simple ideas work well and involve a minimum of mess! Others are better for older children or adults.

*Suitable for young children, also for the special child*

1-Using the white wax crayon which comes with many egg-decorating kits, write a name on the uncolored egg. Or draw a simple design on it. Dye the egg. The part covered by the crayon will stay white; the rest of the egg will be colored. (If you are supervising the dyeing of eggs with a group of small children, the judicious use of this technique is one of the best trouble preventers. Nobody can argue about the ownership of an egg if a name or initials settles the matter.)

2-Dye the egg any color you like. Decorate it with paste-on seals, loose-leaf binder reinforcement rings, stars, or any-

53

thing else gluable you happen to have on hand. If there is nothing else around, use cancelled postage stamps.

3-Select a simple design. Draw it on the dyed egg with liquid glue. Allow the glue to become slightly tacky. Sprinkle the glue with glitter. Or, spread a thin layer of glue over the entire surface of an uncolored egg, doing one half at a time. Sprinkle the wet glue with glitter.

4-Use felt marking pens to draw designs on the eggs. You may use colored pens on white eggs, black pens on colored eggs, or any other combination you like.

CAUTION     Be careful about using felt marking pens on eggs which will be used for food. The ink sometimes bleeds through the eggshell. Cooked egg which has gotten felt pen ink on it should not be eaten.

5-Paint designs on the eggs with watercolor or tempera paints. This is a popular way to decorate Easter eggs in many parts of the world.

6-Draw designs on the eggs with colored crayons. This is a wonderful way for preschoolers to decorate eggs.

7-Cut out tiny flowers from discarded seed catalogs or small designs from scraps of wallpaper. Glue these on white or colored eggs.

8-Cut tiny flowers, animals, or other designs from scraps of pretty cloth. Dampen them *slightly* to make them cling more closely to the surface. Glue them to the egg.

## STRIPED, PLAID, AND CHECKED EGGS

Eggs may be striped in several ways. Plaid and checked eggs are made by repeating the striping both ways on the egg.

### Materials

> White eggs, preferably hardcooked for easier handling
> Rubber bands, large enough to fit snugly around the egg, in the width you want. Or, masking tape.
> Egg dyes in two or three colors which combine well, or, several shades of the same color
> Egg holder
> For some methods:
> white wax crayon
> gummed stars

### Simple Striped or Banded Eggs

1-Prepare two colors of egg dye. One should be either a darker shade of the first color, or, a color which, used over the first, produces a third, pleasing color. For colors which may be combined in this way, see page 45.

2-Dip the whole egg into the first and lightest color dye. Let the egg dry.

3-Put the egg into the egg holder. Dip the egg into the second color dye only as far up as the wire egg holder comes. When the dipped part of the egg is the shade you want, take it out of the dye. Let the egg dry with freshly dyed side down so that the color will not run.

4-When the egg is dry, repeat step three on the other end of the egg. You will have an egg with dark ends and a lighter band in the middle.

### Rubber-band or Tape Striped Eggs

1-Prepare two or more colors of egg dye. See the directions above under simple striped or banded eggs for more information about how to do this.

2-Dip the whole egg in light colored egg dye. Let it dry.

3-Put rubber bands or masking tape around the dyed egg where you want your stripes to be. Be sure to use bands which fit snugly but not tightly. You may want to use all wide bands or all narrow bands or a combination of them.

4-Dip the egg in the second color dye. Remove the egg when it is the shade you want, and let it dry. Then remove the bands.

5-Stripes in two colors are very attractive, but if you want more, an additional cup of egg dye will be needed for each new color. Repeat step 3 and 4, using the rubber bands or masking tape to protect the first stripes, and also to mark off new ones. Remove them when the egg is finished.

6-If you want white stripes on a dark egg, put the rubber bands or masking tape on a white egg, then dip the egg in a dark-colored dye. Let the egg dry, then remove the bands.

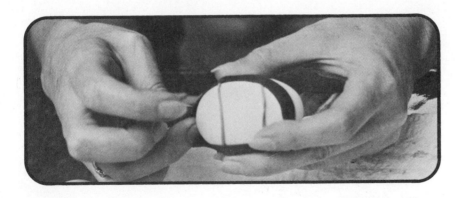

## Checked Eggs

Checked eggs are made the same way as striped eggs, *except* wide bands are used. Use some to form strips lengthwise around the egg, then put the rubber bands or masking tape around the width of the egg to form checks. Dip the egg in the dye bath until the desired color is obtained. If you want a colored egg with white checks, start with the bands on a white egg, then dip the egg in one color dye. Let the egg dry. Remove the bands.

If you want colored checks on a darker background, dye the whole egg in a light color before putting the bands in place. Then dip the egg in darker egg dye.

## Plaid Eggs

Plaid eggs are a more complicated form of striped eggs. The materials used are the same. These eggs should not be attempted by young children. They are too difficult to do.

1-Work out a simple plaid. For best results, it should contain white and not more than two colors.

2-Outline the parts of the plaid you want white by covering these areas on the egg with rubber bands or masking tape. Do it in the same way you did for rubber-band striped eggs.

57

3-Dip the egg in the lightest color dye. Let it dry. Remove the bands.

4-With the white wax crayon, cover up the parts of the plaid you want to stay white.

5-Repeat step 2, but this time cover up the parts of the plaid you want to remain the lighest color.

6-Repeat step 3, except this time dip the egg in the next color dye.

7-You may stop here if you wish or you may repeat steps 2, 3, and 4. Remember, plaid eggs are more effective if they are kept simple.

### All-American Eggs

Follow any of the striped-egg methods using red and blue coloring to produce an egg which is red on one end, blue on the other, with a narrow white strip in the middle. Decorate the egg with gummed silver stars.

# TIE-DYED EASTER EGGS

Teen-agers love these colorful and interesting eggs. They make an especially good project for a junior high or high school art class or for a Scout troop. There is a sense of excitement in coming to class the next day and discovering what the finished egg actually looks like. Tie-dyed eggs may also be used with children much younger than teen-agers, and sometimes they have particular appeal for use with the special child.

*Suitable for young children and the special child*

## Materials

White eggs, hardcooked
Piece of cotton cloth about 5 inches by 6 inches for each
    egg (part of a worn-out bedsheet is ideal)
2 small rubber bands for each egg
Egg dye—allow 1 cup of dye solution for at least every 2 eggs
Vinegar

## Method

1-Prepare the egg dye according to directions given on the
    package.
2-Roll each egg in a piece of dry cloth.
3-Gather the cloth together at each end of the egg and
    fasten, tightly, close to each end of the egg with a rubber
    band. You will have an egg which resembles one of the
    poppers used as favors at parties.

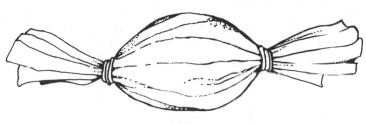

4-Dip the cloth-wrapped egg in the egg coloring. Get the cloth thoroughly wet with the coloring.

5-Put the egg aside to dry overnight, still wrapped in the cloth.

6-The next day, unwrap your tie-dyed egg and see what you have.

*Rainbow eggs*

## RAINBOW EGGS

*Suitable for special child*

Rainbow or variegated eggs are very easy to make and are exceptionally attractive. You never know quite what you will get until the egg is unwrapped.

### Materials

Piece of thin cotton cloth about 6 inches square
Eyedropper
Egg dyes in any 3 colors you like
Vinegar
Up to 6 eggs, preferably hardcooked for easier handling

60

# Easter Eggs with Dye

*Method*

1-Using a separate container for each color dye dissolve the dye in two teaspoonfuls of water. Check with the dye package to see if you should use hot or cold water. Add 2 or 3 drops of vinegar to each container of dye.

2-Slightly dampen the piece of cloth. Wrap it completely around one egg.

3-Using the eyedropper, drop spots of dye on the cloth-wrapped egg. Rinse the dropper and repeat with the second color dye. Rinse the dropper again and repeat with the third color.

4-Twist the dye-spotted cloth tightly around the egg so the colors run together to produce a rainbow or variegated effect.

5-Unwrap the eggs to see what has happened.

6-Rinse out the cloth and wring it well so that it is almost dry before using it to do other eggs.

**COMIC STRIP EGGS**

This simple technique produces very attractive results. Young children will have better results if they do it with white paste instead of the harder-to-use liquid white glue.

*Suitable for young children*

61

Easter Eggs For Everyone

*Materials*

Hardcooked white eggs
Egg dye
Comic strips featuring favorite characters
White paste or all-purpose white glue
Scissors

*Method*

1-Dye the eggs bright, solid colors. For really vivid shades, use double-strength dye.
2-Cut out pictures of comic strip characters. You may want to use Dick Tracy, Peanuts, or anyone else you like. Just be sure they will fit on the egg.
3-Paste or glue the cut-outs on the eggs. Smooth out any wrinkles.

**LEAF-DECORATED EGGS**

Leaf-decorated Easter eggs are often seen in Austria. They have a delicate design on a solid color background. Be sure to use very fine thread to bind on the leaves, otherwise there will be noticeable marks on the finished eggs.

### Easter Eggs with Dye

*Materials*

    Small leaves
    Fine thread
    Onion skins, about 1 cup of skins for 6 eggs
    Uncooked white eggs
    Pot or pan large enough to hold eggs, onion skins, and
        water to cover both—preferably steel, enamel, or glass

*Method*

1-Gather small leaves with interesting shapes. These may be
    from houseplants, weeds, or very young tree leaves.
    Be careful about gathering leaves out of doors in early
    spring, you might accidentally get young Poison Ivy.

*CAUTION*

2-Wash the leaves.
3-While they are still wet, arrange them on the uncooked
    eggs. Fasten in place with the fine thread.
4-Put the eggs in a pan and completely cover them with
    water.
5-Add about 1 cup of onion skins.
6-Cook the eggs over low heat for about 20 minutes.
7-Remove from the heat and rinse the eggs with cold water.
8-Remove the thread and leaves from each egg. You will have
    a stenciled white design on a brown background.

## BLOCKED EGGS

    This is a German variation of leaf-decorated eggs. The use
of the nylon stocking or gauze gives a slightly textured appearance to the surface of the eggs.

# Easter Eggs For Everyone

## Materials

Hardcooked white eggs
Small flowers, leaves, grasses, etc.
Salad oil or uncooked eggwhite
Discarded nylon stocking or piece of fine gauze or
    cheesecloth
String
Egg dye
Vinegar

## Method

1-Wash the flowers, leaves, or grasses. Dry between layers of
    paper toweling.
2-Dip them into a small amount of salad oil or into slightly
    beaten eggwhite.
3-Arrange on the surface of the eggs.
4-Slip a 6-inch section of discarded nylon stocking or a piece of
    gauze over each egg, and tie the ends close to the egg.
5-Prepare the egg dye according to directions given on the
    package.
6-Dye the stocking- or gauze-wrapped eggs until they are the
    shades you like.
7-Remove the wrapping and leaves from each egg.

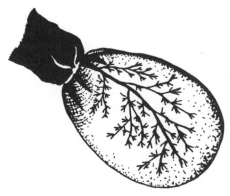

# SASSY EASTER EGGS

Sassy Easter eggs are adapted from an old Dutch method for leaf-decorated eggs, which had its origins in the Saxon traditions in the eastern part of the Netherlands.

## Materials

Tiny leaves and young field flowers—the more variety the better
Piece of white cotton cloth about 8" square for each egg.
For each egg the skins from 3 or 4 medium onions
White string
About 1 cup of coffee grounds
Uncooked white eggs.

## Method

1-Place a square of cloth on a table and cover it with a layer of onion skins.
2-On it arrange in a pleasing pattern leaves and flowers of all kinds. Use a few colored flowers if you can find them.
3-Place an uncooked egg in the middle and take up the cloth by the four corners. Do this very carefully so that everything stays in place. Cover the egg completely.
4-Tie the covering on the egg with the cotton string. Fasten it well so that the bundle will stay together.
5-Put the bundle in a medium or large saucepan and completely cover it with water. Add the coffee grounds.
6-Boil the wrapped eggs gently for about 20 minutes. Let stand until cool enough to handle.
7-Unwrap the bundles and see what you have. There should be some yellow from the onion skins, brown from the coffee, and white and colored shapes where the leaves and flowers were bound against the eggs.
8-If you like, rub the finished egg with a piece of bacon to make it shine.

## SCRATCH-CARVED EGGS

Scratch-carving is one of the oldest ways of decorating Easter eggs. The designs may be very simple or extremely elaborate. The skill of the artist is a major consideration. Scratch-carved eggs are still very popular, and simple ones are quite easy to make.

### Materials

Hardcooked eggs, dyed solid colors. Bright or dark colors are the most effective. A design will not show up properly against a light background.
Needle or a knife with a fine, sharp point.

### Method

1-Work out your design on a piece of paper. A beginner might like to try a name, initial, or a simple flower. If you are a skilled artist, there is almost no limit to what you can do.
2-Pencil the design very lightly on the egg.
3-Using the needle or the point of the knife, scratch the design into the eggshell. You will have a white design on a colored egg.

## SCRATCH-CARVED VARIATION

This variation of the scratch-carving technique produces a colored design on a white egg.

*Materials*

    Hardcooked white eggs
    Melted wax or a candle
    Egg dye
    Vinegar
    Needle, knife, or other sharp instrument
    Few drops of oil, if desired

*Method*

1-Dip hardcooked eggs in the melted wax until they are completely covered. Or, light the candle and carefully dribble the melting wax over the egg until the entire surface is covered.
2-Allow the wax to harden.
3-While the wax hardens, work out some simple designs.
4-With the needle, knife, or other sharp instrument, scratch the design through the wax on the surface of the egg. Be sure you cut deeply enough to reach the eggshell.

5-Following the directions on your dye package, dissolve one color of dye in a cup of water and add vinegar as specified.

6-Place the carved egg in the cooled dye bath and leave it there until the carved sections have reached the desired shade.

7-Remove the egg from the dye bath and dry it.

8-Place the scratch-carved eggs in a flat pan lined with paper toweling. Put pan in a warm oven for a few minutes until the wax is softened.

9-With a soft cloth or paper towel, wipe off the softened wax. If desired, polish the egg with a few drops of cooking oil.

# bAtik pROCESS EGGS

Batik is an old Javanese method of decorating cloth. Melted wax is applied to the fabric with a special tool called a *tjanting,* and the cloth is dipped in dye. The part which has been covered with the wax resists the dye and remains the original color. If several colors are desired, more wax is applied and the cloth dyed again, this time using a color which can be used successfully over the first one. For example, blue dyed over yellow will result in green.

With some variations, both in the exact method of wax application and in the tool used in the process, the batik technique is often employed in the decoration of Easter eggs. All of the eggs in this section are batik-process eggs.

## ETCHED EGGS

The Macedonians were skillful Easter egg etchers. They boiled the eggs in logwood dye to make them red. When the eggs were cool, threads of wax were placed on them by hand. Then the eggs were boiled again in sour whey or in a citric acid solution. This bleached off all of the color except where the wax threads had been applied.

## Easter Eggs For Everyone

You can still etch Easter eggs even if you do not have logwood or sour whey. There are several ways to do them. Most of the things you need should be found in your kitchen.

### Materials

White eggs, hardcooked and dyed any bright or dark solid color you like. A light color will not show up well when the egg is etched.

To make the designs use one of these:

white wax crayon

ordinary candle—birthday candles work best

pin stylus (see page 40) and beeswax candle.

To bleach the egg use one of these combinations:

1 teaspoonful of household chlorine bleach mixed in 1 cup of cool water

1 tablespoonful of baking soda mixed in 1 cup of cool water

1 tablespoonful of citric acid crystals (available in most drugstores) dissolved in ¼ cup hot water. Add cool water to make 1 cup.

# Batik Process Eggs

## *Method*

1-Draw a simple design on the dyed egg with the white wax crayon, the candle, or the pin stylus and beeswax. Or, dribble blobs of wax on the egg by holding the lighted candle over it and letting the melting wax drip onto the surface of the egg. This gives a hit-and-miss pattern. If you use any of the methods using melted wax, let the wax harden for a few minutes before bleaching the egg.

2-Put the egg into the bleaching solution and leave it there until the color bleaches off. It will take anywhere from two minutes to ten minutes or slightly longer. If you are using the citric acid solution, the egg will become covered with tiny bubbles, and a skin will form on the egg. When you rub the skin, the dye on the unwaxed portion will come off.

3-If desired, place the egg in a paper-lined pan and heat slightly in a barely warm oven until the wax softens. With a soft cloth, rub off the wax. Or, you may leave the wax on the egg. It won't harm its appearance.

# PYSANKY AND KRASHANKY

Some of the most beautiful Easter eggs in the world origi-- nate in the Slavic nations. In the Ukraine, Poland, Czecho- slovakia, and other countries of Central Europe, there are two kinds of Easter eggs. One is a solid, brilliantly colored hard- boiled egg which may be eaten. The Ukrainians call these eggs *krashanky* from a word which means "color." Krashanky are often dyed red in honor of the blood which Christ shed on the cross at Calvary. These are the eggs which are used to break the long Lenten fast, for exchange with one's friends, and in Easter games. Many peasants believe that krashanky have healing powers. They also use them to ward off certain kinds of evil.

Another traditional style of Easter eggs, *pysanky*, are fre- quently exquisite works of art. This process gets its name from a Ukrainian verb, *pysaty* "to write." This describes how the eggs are decorated: The designs are literally written on the eggs with special stylus dipped in melted beeswax. The pro- cess is closely related to batik.

The art of pysanky actually goes back well before the be- ginnings of Christianity. Although records date no further back than the thirteenth century, many of the motifs, or characteristic design patterns, have been traced to the neo- lithic age.

For centuries the Ukrainians have been an agricultural people. Everything they did has been related to nature and the fertility of their land. The sun, as a power, was all- important to them, and the egg was regarded as a symbol of it.

To the very early Ukrainians, pysanky combined the power of the sun and the spirit worlds—or life and death. Pysanky were used in the spring, when the sun came to melt the winter's snow, and life of all kinds returned to the Steppes.

In 988 Christian missionaries arrived in the Ukraine carry- ing with them a startling new message of life and death. A completely different dimension was added to the old meaning of the eggs: The Son took the place of the sun, and pysanky became deeply religious in symbolism. This time the religion was Christianity.

According to an old legend, the Virgin Mary decorated some pysanky to offer to Pontius Pilate when she pleaded for her Son's life. As she prepared them, her tears fell on the eggs, forming dots of vivid color. When Mary went before Pilate, she fell to her knees in grief. As she did, the pysanky rolled from her apron across the floor and continued to roll until they were distributed around the world. Even today, one type of pysanky are called "teardrop eggs."

Among some Ukrainians, there is still the belief that the fate of the world depends on pysanky. As long as egg-decorating continues, the world will exist. Should the custom cease, evil, in the guise of an ancient, vicious monster chained to a huge cliff, will encompass the world and destroy it. Each year the monster's servants encircle the globe, keeping track of the number of pysanky made. When there are few, the monster's chains loosen, and evil flows through the world. When there are many, his chains hold taut, allowing love to conquer evil.

In countries where pysanky are made, each region has its own rituals, symbols, and dye formulas for the eggs. These are carefully preserved and are passed along from one generation to the next. In some parts of the United States, women still decorate pysanky as their grandmothers did in Europe.

When Ukrainians began moving to the Canadian prairies, they adapted the old pysanky-making traditions to their new way of life. Indelible pencils are frequently used in the coloring process, the metal tabs from feed and grain store calendars moved into new roles as tips for the styluses, and stalks or sheaves of wheat, characteristic of the new homeland, have become prominent pysanky motifs. Canadian pysanky-making is becoming much more precise and artistically related to

73

everyday life. And Canadian pysanky-makers take their art so seriously that each year a psyanky competition is held in Edmonton in which the eggs are rigidly judged according to the purity of the traditional Ukrainian design. In Canada, to cut down the breakage problem, wooden pysanky have become popular.

Though the meanings of the designs vary from place to place, certain motifs are characteristically used in the pysanky of a particular area. A trained person can often tell where an egg originated just by looking at the designs used. For example, the pysanky of the Great Steppes feature baroque, floral patterns, while geometrics often appear on eggs coming from the Carpathian Mountains.

Because the women take great pride in the originality of their pysanky, the eggs are usually decorated in secrecy; nobody wants her ideas copied. No two eggs are ever exactly alike. Pysanky are seen in public for the first time when they are taken to the church to be blessed along with other Paschal food on Easter Eve.

Pysanky were originally dyed with vegetable colors supplemented with an occasional bit of chemical pigment, but most people in the United States use commercial dyes now. Ordinary fabric dyes work well if they are used in a strong solution, or you may prefer to order regular pysanky dye. These are not expensive and may be a good investment if you plan to try pysanky. Some of these dyes are safe for food while others are not. Check the individual containers to see which ones are edible.

The different colors have special significance when they are used for making pysanky. Green means money; purple, high power; orange, attraction; black, remembrance; blue, health; brown, happiness; white, purity; red, love; pink, success; and yellow, spirituality.

Pysanky are never made from cooked eggs. Instead, either blown or uncooked eggs are used. If you plan to keep your pysanky for a long time, it is best to use blown eggs.

74

## Batik Process Eggs

Regardless of where pysanky originate, there are certain designs which are commonly used in decorating them. The significance may change from village to village, but the basic motifs remain much the same. Pysanky designs are usually intended to *suggest* a thing rather than picture it exactly. They are divided into classifications: geometric, plant, and animals and other creatures. These are some of the more frequently seen pysanky designs. Keep them in mind when planning your own eggs.

### *Geometric*

Checkerboard or sieve. This is used for filling in borders.

Circle, poppy, and spiderweb. They represent the sun and are the symbols of good fortune.

The Cross. This is religious today, but was originally a pagan symbol.

Dots. These may be specks, circles, or ovals. They are used for stars or for Mary's tears.

Horns, bends, spirals, and maidens

Ladders. These are used as filler with other designs, especially crosses. They are never seen alone.

Little baskets

Ribbon or belt. This means eternity.

Spoons and leaves. Spoons stand alone, while leaves come in twos and threes.

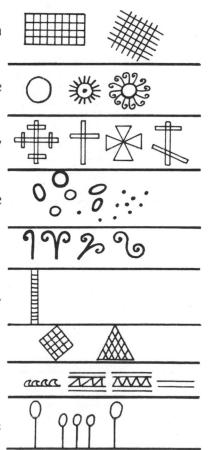

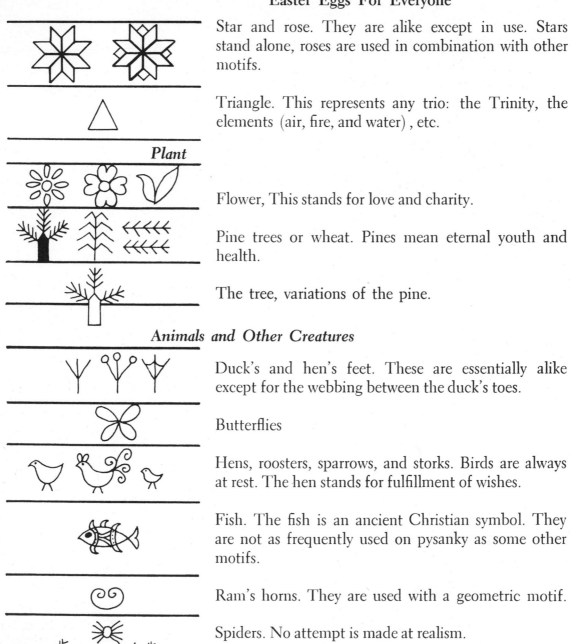

Star and rose. They are alike except in use. Stars stand alone, roses are used in combination with other motifs.

Triangle. This represents any trio: the Trinity, the elements (air, fire, and water), etc.

### Plant

Flower, This stands for love and charity.

Pine trees or wheat. Pines mean eternal youth and health.

The tree, variations of the pine.

### Animals and Other Creatures

Duck's and hen's feet. These are essentially alike except for the webbing between the duck's toes.

Butterflies

Hens, roosters, sparrows, and storks. Birds are always at rest. The hen stands for fulfillment of wishes.

Fish. The fish is an ancient Christian symbol. They are not as frequently used on pysanky as some other motifs.

Ram's horns. They are used with a geometric motif.

Spiders. No attempt is made at realism.

Horse or reindeer. These symbolize wealth and prosperity.

76

## Batik Process Eggs

Regardless of the technique used, all pysanky-making begins by dividing the egg into sections or fields, with the basic lines running lengthwise and/or crosswise around the egg. These segments are sometimes made with a single line, but more often a double or triple line is used. The entire design is based on these divisions which separate the individual motifs. The motifs are repeated in multiples of two and from two to forty repetitions may be used on a single egg. Seconday divisions are formed by single lines separating the original sections into smaller fields in which individual parts of the design are placed. Pysanky may also be divided in half horizontally with the design centered on either end. Or, an egg may be decorated in the form of a barrel with a wheel at either end and a cylinder in the middle.

Unless you have an exceptionally steady hand and much experience in the art, use a rubber band or masking tape placed around the egg to guide you in marking the divisions. Or use very light pencil marks. Do not attempt to erase pencil marks. You will only smudge the egg.

For each method, beeswax is needed. This is used instead of paraffin because it has a high melting point, gives better coverage, and has a greater resistance to dyes. Lines made with melted beeswax are even and do not smear easily. Though beeswax candles can be made at home, this is a tedious process. Bought ones can be expensive. If you attend a church which uses beeswax candles, perhaps you could persuade your pastor to let you have one or two stubs. Or, heat your stylus in an ordinary candle flame and quickly press it against a cake of dressmaker's beeswax. This can be found in any store carrying sewing supplies. One cake is inexpensive and will last for a long time.

If you have never made pysanky before, it is a good idea to begin with teardrop eggs. Use a pin stylus (see p. 40), which is much easier to handle than a pysanky stylus.

For making traditional pysanky a pysanky stylus will be needed. Called a kistka, the stylus may be purchased with

77

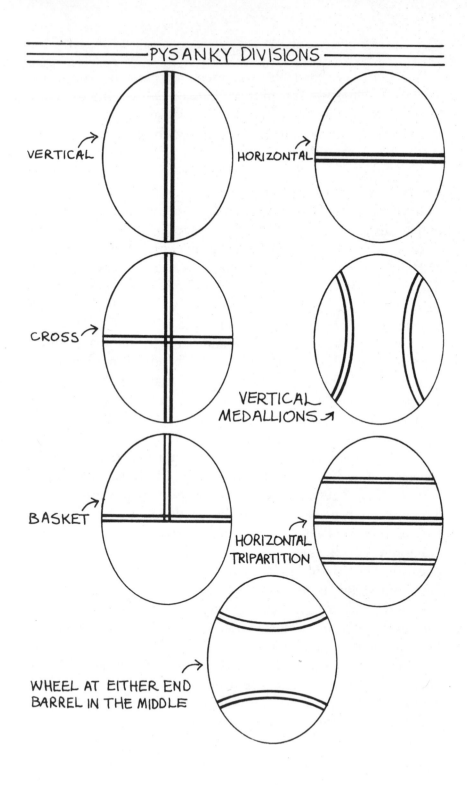

# PYSANKY DIVISIONS

VERTICAL

HORIZONTAL

CROSS

VERTICAL MEDALLIONS

BASKET

HORIZONTAL TRIPARTITION

WHEEL AT EITHER END
BARREL IN THE MIDDLE

fine, medium, or heavy point and may be ordered by mail at a modest price. Or, you can make a pysanky-type stylus. For lines of varying widths you will want to make (or buy) several styluses with different sized openings in the cones.

# HOW TO MAKE A KISTKA OR PSYANKY STYLUS

## *Materials*

Freshly cut straight stick about 6 inches long and ¼ inch thick (Dry wood will catch fire.)

*CAUTION*

A piece of brass shim stock about ½ inch long and ¾ inch wide. This thin brass foil comes in rolls 6 inches wide and can be cut with scissors. Automotive supply houses carry it.

Needle

Sharp penknife

Very fine wire—a piece about 10 inches long.

## *Method*

1-Wrap the brass shim tightly around the needle so that you have a tube ½ inch long with an opening in each end. Slip the shim tube off the needle and set aside.

2-With the knife, cut a narrow V-shaped wedge into one end of the stick. Make the cut about ¼ inch deep. Work carefully so that you do not split the stick or cut yourself.

79

3-Fit the brass tube into the V in the stick. It should fit tightly in the narrow end of the cut. Leave about ⅛ inch of the tube above the stick on one end and have a larger amount of the tube showing below the stick.

4-With the wire, wrap over and under the tube, using a figure-8 motion to fasten the tube firmly in place in the V. Twist the ends of the wire together.

A stand of some kind is useful in making pysanky. You may, use the core from a roll of transparent tape, the core of a carbon typewriter ribbon, the upside-down top from a pill bottle, or the upside-down top from certain salt and pepper shakers. If you use one of these, be sure it is at least 1 inch across. Or, you can make a stand by placing 3 thumbtacks in a small piece of corrugated cardboard so that they form a triangle with sides about 1 inch long.

In decorating pysanky, you must apply the colors in a certain order if they are to remain bright. Using a small brush, a toothpick, or similar tool, fill in the areas which are to be green or blue with dye of that color. Do this first. Then cover these areas with wax before going on with the egg. Begin with yellow, go on to orange, then light red, dark red, violet, and black. In order to get the proper depth of color with a few shades, it will be necessary for the egg to remain in the dye bath for a long time. If the last color on an egg is black, it is often necessary to keep the egg in the dye overnight. When you are working with a blown egg which needs to stay in the dye bath for a long time, let the egg fill up with the dye. It will get so heavy that it will stay under the dye without coming to the surface. When the color is right, carefully shake out the dye which is inside the egg.

There are many different pysanky techniques. These are just a few, arranged in order of difficulty.

If you have never worked with a stylus before, practice on a spare egg before you begin work on the egg you plan to glamorize. It takes practice to know the correct temperature for the stylus and the right way to handle it.

# TEARDROP EGGS

Teardrop eggs are an authentic form of pysanky. They are frequently made by Slavic women who feel that they lack the time or skill to do the more intricate forms of pysanky. Since they do not require the complicated equipment needed for the more elaborate types and the designs are simpler, teardrop eggs provide a good introduction to the art. These lovely eggs may be done quite successfully by children as young as ten or eleven.

*Suitable for children 10 and up*

## Materials

> Blown white eggs.
> Egg dyes in one or more colors, plus black. (Use fabric dye in a strong solution for black, if you cannot find black egg dye.)
> Pin stylus
> Beeswax candle, or, wax candle and block of dressmaker's beeswax
> Rubber bands or masking tape
> Pencil
> Something for a base. Use a core from a roll of tape, a carbon typewriter ribbon core, or one of the other things suggested on page 80.

## Method

1-Using the tape or rubber band as a guide, draw lines *very lightly* to divide the surface of the egg first into halves length-wise, then into crosswise halves. Do this with the pencil. You will have an egg marked off into 4 sections. The penciled lines must be barely dark enough for you to see them, but not so dark that they will be visible when the egg is dyed. The lines cannot be removed without spoiling the egg.

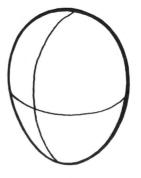

2-If you are using a wax candle and a block of dressmaker's beeswax, heat the tip of the pin stylus in the candle flame for a few seconds or until it becomes very hot. Then press the hot tip against the block of beeswax. The head of the pin will pick up a small quantity of melted beeswax. If you are using a beeswax candle, heat the tip of the stylus in the candle flame, then dip it in the pool of melted wax at the base of the flame.

3-Using the lengthwise penciled line as a guide, touch the wax-filled tip of the stylus to the surface of the egg in a quick stroke, diagonal to the line. Quickly pull the stylus away. The mark should be in the shape of a teardrop. This is your basic stroke. With a little practice you will be able to do it rapidly.

4-Reheat the stylus and dip it again in the melted beeswax. Repeat the diagonal teardrop stroke quite close to the first mark on the egg. Do this all the way around the egg. You will probably need to reheat and redip the stylus for every stroke you make.

5-Repeat the process, making diagonal marks across the first ones and going the opposite way around the egg. You will have a band which looks like an uneven cross-stitch. Do not be concerned if your marks look a bit smoky.

6-Dip the egg into the lightest color of dye. The waxed marks will remain white. Leave the wax on the egg.

7-Using the same technique, mark out a simple cross on the front and back of the egg. Again use X-shaped marks.

8-Dip the egg in the black dye. Leave it there until the egg is a deep black. The amount of time this takes will depend on the strength of your dye. If necessary, leave the egg in the dye overnight. Since you are using blown eggs, you will need to keep pushing the egg under the dye. If the egg has to stay in the dye overnight, place something light on the egg to keep it under the solution. Touching just the waxed parts, this will not mar the egg.

## Batik Process Eggs

One of the plastic carbon typewriter ribbon cores will work well. So will the core from a roll of tape. Or, allow the hollow egg to fill with dye. Its own weight will keep it under the dye solution. You can shake out the excess dye when the egg is finished.

9-When the final color—black here—is dark enough, remove the egg from the dye bath and dry it with a soft cloth.

10-Hold the egg just to the side of a candle flame so that the wax softens, a section at a time. Do not hold the egg in the flame because that will cause a layer of soot to form on the egg. When the wax is soft, wipe that section off with a soft cloth and go on to the next section. Do this until the wax is off the entire egg. Or, follow step 21 for traditional pysanky (page 90).

11-Polish the egg with a soft cloth. You will have a black egg with a white band lengthwise around it and a colored cross on either side.

# TEARDROP EGG VARIATION

CAUTION
Because the Crayola used in this technique must be heated to near the smoking point, this method is intended for use only by highly responsible older children under supervision or by adults. Never permit younger children to attempt it.

## Materials

Blown eggs
Egg dye in one color, preferably light
Pin stylus
Crayola in a dark color or a medium shade which harmonizes with the egg dye
A low, flat tin can or other similar container for melted Crayola. Be sure it is very clean. The can and Crayola do not go directly on the heat.
Small pot or pan for heating water. Use one large enough to hold the tin can in water about ¾ inch deep.

## Method

1-Dye the eggs.
2-Break up the Crayola and put the pieces in the clean can.
3-Place the can in the pan of water and heat over a low flame until the Crayola is melted and almost smoking hot. Be extremely careful that the Crayola does not catch fire.

CAUTION

4-When the Crayola has melted, remove the pan from the heat but leave the can in the pan of water. If the Crayola begins to harden as you work, reheat.
5-Using the pin stylus and the same technique as you did in teardrop eggs, follow the design you have marked lightly with pencil on the egg. Do the entire design in the one color with the melted Crayola.

Batik Process Eggs

6-Do not remove the hardened Crayola from the egg when you have completed your design. The texture of the wax on the surface of the egg is an important part of the decoration.

7-If you prefer, the same method may be used with brightly colored melted Crayola on a white egg.

## SIMPLIFIED PYSANKY

This modified version of the traditional pysanky is particularly good for use with anyone who should not use a lighted candle. It is another excellent introduction to the art for children as young as nine or for some retarded youths. The results are lovely. A white wax crayon is recommended, but other colors may be used if you prefer.

*Suitable for ages 9 and up and for some special youth*

*Materials*

    Hardcooked white eggs at room temperature
White wax crayon
Liquid food coloring. Do not use a color which must be mixed.
Vinegar—2 teaspoonfuls for each cup of dye
Cup of water
Rubber band or masking tape which will fit around the egg as line guide

*Method*

1-Choose a simple pysanky design. Work it out on paper until you have a pretty design which will fit on your egg. A simple star with a border of wheat works very well.

85

2-Using the tape or rubber band to help you draw straight lines on the egg, take the white wax crayon and draw in the parts of the design that you want to have white.

3-In a cup, combine the water and the vinegar. Add enough liquid food coloring to dye the egg a light color. A few drops of food coloring should be right.

4-Using an egg holder or a tablespoon, put the egg in the dye bath. When it is the shade you want it, remove the egg and dry it with a paper towel or a soft cloth.

5-Using the tape or rubber band to help you draw straight lines, take the white wax crayon and draw in the part of the design you want to have stay the light color.

6-Add more food coloring of the same color to the dye bath so that you get a darker shade of that color.

7-Put the egg in the dye bath again. Leave it there until it is as dark as you want it to be. Remove the tape and you will have an egg in white and two shades of the same color.

If you wish, you can repeat the process a third time, but if you stop after step 7, you have a very attractive egg. Or, instead of adding more food coloring of the same color to the dye bath after the egg has been dipped once, you may add a second color which will produce a third, pleasing color when added to the first one. See page 45 for colors which may be combined.

# TRADITIONAL PYSANKY

The pysanka illustrated incorporates some of the traditional design elements in the use of the endless line, the triangles, the dots, and the stars. Yet it is easy for a beginner to do.

## Materials

> Blown white egg
> Narrow masking tape or rubber band
> Pysanky stylus
> Candle
> Cake of dressmaker's beeswax
> Tablespoon
> Egg dye in yellow, red, and black

## Method

1-Light the candle and seal the blowing holes in each end of the egg with a drop or two of melted wax. Put the candle in a holder of some sort so that it is firmly in place while you work.

2-Put a ¼ inch strip of tape crosswise around the center circumference of the egg. Or, you may use rubber bands.

3-Heat the point of the stylus in the candle flame for about 15 seconds, then press it against the cake of beeswax.

4-Test the flow of wax from the stylus by making a mark with it on a piece of paper or your fingernail. If you test the stylus on your fingernail, be careful not to burn yourself. The wax is hot. The wax should flow smoothly and not blot. A blot is very difficult to handle, but it can be removed with houschold cleaning fluid. *CAUTION*

5-With the stylus draw a line around the egg on either side of the tape to make two lines ¼ inch apart. Let the wax

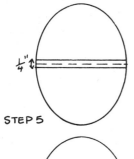

STEP 5

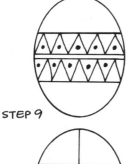

STEP 6 + 7

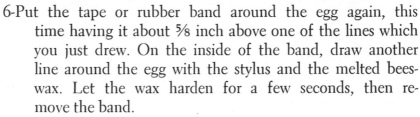

harden a few seconds, then remove the tape or rubber bands.

6-Put the tape or rubber band around the egg again, this time having it about ⅝ inch above one of the lines which you just drew. On the inside of the band, draw another line around the egg with the stylus and the melted beeswax. Let the wax harden for a few seconds, then remove the band.

7-Repeat step 6 on the other side of the inner belt.

8-With the stylus and beeswax, but working freehand, draw an even number of triangles between the lines forming the wide bands around the egg. Let the wax harden for a few seconds.

9-Put a dot of wax in the center of each triangle in the two rows with their bases along the inner belt.

10-Put a piece of tape or a rubber band around the egg, dividing it in half length-wise. With the stylus and melted beeswax draw a line across the end of the egg, from the lines drawn in steps 6 and 7, over the end, to the band on the other side. Do this at each end of the egg.

11-Put the tape or rubber band lengthwise around the egg again, to divide it in half at right angles to the first vertical division. Using the band as a guide, mark both ends of the egg into fourths as shown in the diagram. With the stylus and melted beeswax, draw in this line.

12-With the stylus and melted beeswax, but working freehand, draw additional lines as shown in the diagram for this step. Repeat pattern at the other end of the egg.

STEP 8

STEP 9

STEP 10

STEP 12

88

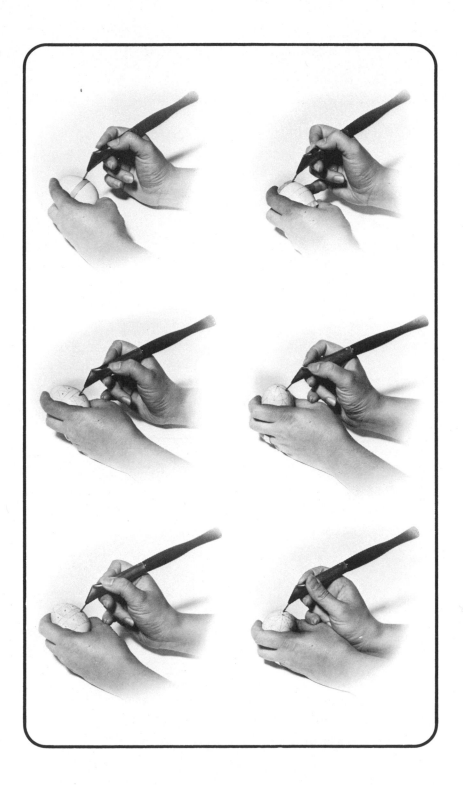

13-Dip the egg in yellow dye, pushing it under with the spoon until it is the shade you want. Remove the egg from the dye bath and dry it.

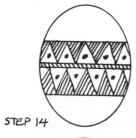

STEP 14

14-With the stylus and melted beeswax, draw short diagonal lines in the two bands of triangles which do not contain dots. Draw diagonal lines also between the two lines of the center belt.

STEP 15

15-With the stylus and wax, cover up the shaded areas as shown in the diagram for this step. A small brush can be used for this, and for other steps when sections of the surface are to be covered.

16-Dip the egg in the red dye and push it under with the spoon until it is the shade you want it to be. Remove it from the dye bath and dry it. The star pattern on the end is now red, and the outer triangles remain yellow.

STEP 17

17-With the stylus and wax, draw an inner star on each end of the egg as shown in the diagram.

18-With the stylus, or brush, and melted wax, cover up all but the inner star on the ends of the egg.

19-With the stylus, or brush, and wax, completely fill in the rows of triangles and the inner belt in which you drew short diagonal lines in step 14. You will have red and yellow lines in the triangles. Now all the egg is covered with wax except the dotted triangles and the inner stars at each end.

STEP 22

20-Place the egg in the black dye and put a scotch tape core or similar weight on it to keep it under the dye. Leave it in the dye overnight.

21-Remove the egg from the dye bath and dry it. Place the egg in a pan lined with paper toweling. Place it in a slightly warm oven for a few minutes. When the wax softens, remove the egg from the oven and wipe off the wax. Or, you may use the method described in step 10 under teardrop eggs (page 83).

22-Admire your own cleverness. You will have a black star on each end of the egg, inside of a larger red star.

Around the middle of the egg will be a narrow band of alternating short red and yellow lines. Outside the narrow band will be wider bands made up of triangles. The outer triangles will be made up of alternating red and yellow lines, and the inner ones will be black with a white dot in the center of each one. The major lines in the design will be white with yellow triangles between the outer star and the belt.

*Some of the collage eggs described in pages 93-129*

# COllAGE EGGS

Collage or scrap-box eggs can be made even when you are absolutely certain that there isn't a thing in the house with egg-decorating possibilities.

Search through boxes of sewing supplies, gather up odd bits of craft materials you might have around, even raid the cleaning cabinet. Have you ever really considered the egg-decorating potential of a copper pot scrubber or used postage stamps or leftover bits of yarn? And what about that pretty scrap of dress fabric you hated to throw out, but which is too small to be of any use?

Turn your imagination loose. Trim, snip, overlap, or even crochet these things together and glue them onto your egg. Use a colored egg as the base and cover only part of it, or cover it all. You never know what might turn out.

## BINSEGRAAS EGGS

Among the Pennsylvania Dutch, one of the early traditional methods of decorating Easter eggs was to use the pith of the *binsegraas*, a rush which grows where the soil is quite damp. The strands of pith were coiled around a paste-covered blown egg until the entire surface of the egg was covered.

# Easter Eggs For Everyone

Then interestingly shaped scraps of calico cloth were pasted on the egg. This technique was out of style for many years until it was revived at the Pennsylvania Dutch Folk Festival in Kutztown, Pennsylvania, in 1958.

Some Polish Easter eggs are also decorated in this manner.

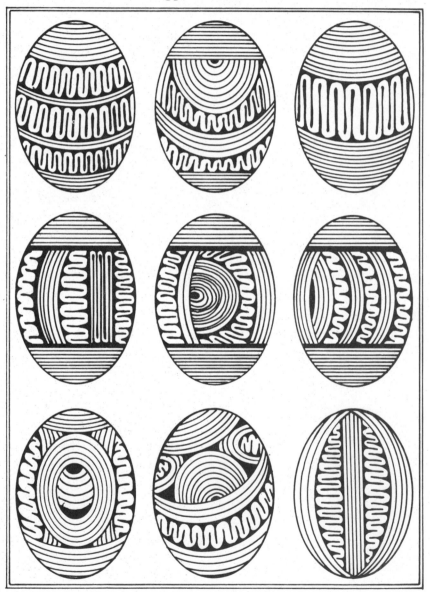

## BINSEGRAAS EGGS—POLISH-STYLE

The artistic Poles have their own way of decorating *binse-graas* eggs. Polish-style eggs are much more elaborate than the ones done by the Pennsylvania Dutch, but the basic method is the same. These eggs are done with rug yarn instead of the rushes, though originally rushes were used.

### Materials

> Blown eggs
> Bits of rug yarn in different colors
> Glue or rubber cement.

### Method

1-Study the illustrations for ideas, then work out a design
    to use on your egg. Small patterns and wavy lines are
    good.

# Easter Eggs For Everyone

2-Apply the glue or rubber cement to one half of the egg.

3-Using the bits of rug yarn, outline the design on this half of the egg.

4-Repeat steps 2 and 3 on the other half.

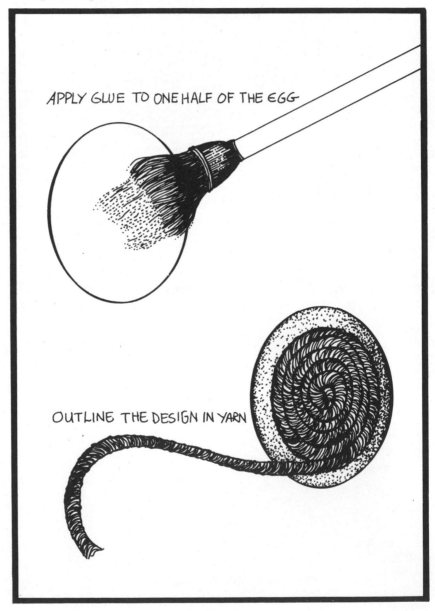

APPLY GLUE TO ONE HALF OF THE EGG

OUTLINE THE DESIGN IN YARN

*Polish-style* binsegraas *eggs*

*Sassy (in center) and leaf-decorated eggs*

## GOLDEN EGGS

These highly sophisticated Easter eggs will appeal to the mature egg crafter who feels that Easter eggs are childish. They may be made from brown eggs since the surface of the egg is covered with paint.

98

# Collage Eggs

## Materials

Blown eggs—brown if you like

Uncooked rice, lentils, small seeds, or miniature forms
of pasta

Liquid white glue or household cement

Tweezers

Small bits of paper

Pencil

Rubber band which will fit around the egg, or masking
tape

Gold paint—preferably spray-on

## Method

1-Tear off bits of paper large enough to cover the blowing
holes in the eggs. (Torn paper will not show as much
as cut paper would.) Glue the bits of paper over the
holes.

2-Lightly pencil a floral, geometric, or other design on the
eggshell. Use the tape or rubber band as a guide in
making straight lines. These designs are most successful
if the egg is first divided into halves, quarters, sixths,
or eighths. Then use the divisions as a guide to your over-
all design.

3-Outline the design with bits of rice, pasta, etc., selecting
whatever will give the best effect. Glue the decorations
on one half of the egg at a time. Use the tweezers to
help you place the design.

4-Allow the egg to dry well.

5-Glue the other half of the design in place.

6-Allow the egg to dry again.

7-When the egg is completely dry, spray or brush on gold
paint.

*Basket of eggs of simple decoration*

*Bowl of striped eggs*

*Comic strip eggs*

*Rainbow or variegated egg*

# JEWELED EGGS

Jeweled eggs and cutout eggs are much like each other in preparation and often in appearance as well. The main difference is that the cutout eggs have a window cut in the shell and a scene inside. Jeweled eggs are left whole after they have been blown. The outside decoration is done in the same way for both types of eggs.

## Materials

Blown white eggs
Egg dye
All-purpose white glue
Tiny beads, sequins, flowers, felt cutouts, etc.
Tweezers
Pencil
Scrap paper

## Method

1-Dye the blown eggs any color you like. Allow them to dry well.
2-Work out a simple design which will be effective with the materials you plan to use. A design based on circles covering the ends or ovals covering the sides of the egg works best.
3-If you cannot do without them, pencil very light guide lines on the eggshell. Try to work without the lines if possible; they will show on the finished egg.
4-Working one row or small section of the design at a time, spot all-purpose glue around the egg. Use tweezers to help you put the tiny decorations in place. Since this type of glue usually dries rapidly, you should be able to go on to the next row immediately.

# CUTOUT EASTER EGGS

These are among the most beautiful of Easter eggs. With a hook attached for hanging, a cutout egg makes a lovely decoration for an egg tree or a Christmas tree. Or, you may prefer to glue a base to the bottom so the egg will stand upright.

## Materials

Blown eggs
Egg dye
Pencil
Darning needle
Manicure scissors—preferably old ones
Colorless nail polish
All-purpose white glue
Tweezers

Use some of these:
  Glitter
  Narrow ribbon, braid, or rickrack
  Florist's clay—a small amount
  Miniature figures
  Tiny beads, sequins, flowers, felt cutouts
  Small brass curtain rings for stand-up eggs
  Small discarded Christmas tree ornament tops for hanging eggs
  Tiny buttons for hanging eggs

## Method

1-Dye the blown eggs and allow them to dry completely.
2-When the eggshells are dry, use a pencil to outline the area to be cut.
3-With the darning needle, make a hole in the eggshell near the pencil line.

*Fabergé exhibit, courtesy Virginia Museum, Richmond.*

*Jeweled egg by Fabergé, courtesy Virginia Museum, Richmond*

Ruth Peek Neely. Cradles made of goose eggs, Easter basket made of an emu egg. Used by permission.

Ruth Peek Neely. Decorated rhea egg, opening at top and bottom, simulated Fabergé style. Used by permission.

Ruth Peek Neely. Two goose eggs—one featuring intricate openings and a small turkey egg inside, the other glowing with fake jewels. Used by permission.

4-Starting at the hole, cut very carefully along the line using the manicure scissors. Use small strokes and keep the points of the scissors turned in, moving the egg as you cut. Cutting the eggshell is not difficult, but it takes patience. Don't worry if the edge of the cut chips slightly or is a bit uneven.

6-Coat the outside of the eggshell with colorless nail polish to strengthen it and add gloss. Let it dry well.

7-If you do not plan to use glitter or sequins on the inside of the eggshell, coat the inside of the shell with colorless nail polish and allow it to dry.

8-If you plan to make a hanging egg, put the hanger in place now. Carefully slip both prongs of a Christmas tree ornament-hanger through the hole in the top of the eggshell. Anchor them in place inside the eggshell by putting them through the holes of a tiny button. Tear a small piece of paper into a circle slightly larger than the button. Glue the paper in place over the button inside the top of the eggshell. Hanging eggs usually

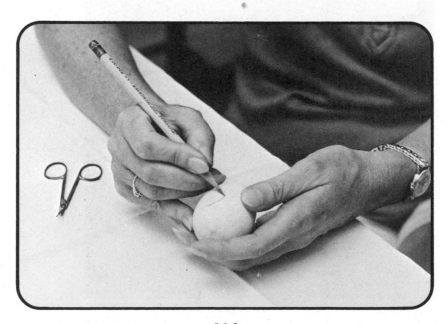

look better if the inside of the shell is finished with glitter or is painted with poster paint after the hanger is in place.

9-To apply glitter to the inside of the egg, coat it thinly with glue, then sprinkle on the glitter. Shake out the extra glitter. Or put a thin coating of glue on the inside of the egg and use tweezers to help you cover the inside of the shell with sequins. Let the egg dry well.

10-For tiny flower arrangements or miniature scenes, first put a piece of florist's clay in the bottom of the egg. With the tweezers, insert the stems of the flowers and leaves or the bottoms of the figures into the clay.

11-Cover the edge of the opening with glitter to match the inside of the egg, or, glue on an edging of narrow ribbon, rickrack, or braid.

12-If you wish, glue tiny felt flowers, beads or sequins to the outside of the egg.

13-For a stand-up egg, glue a small brass curtain ring to the bottom of the egg.

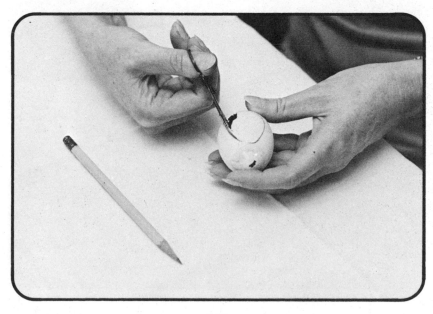

*Cutout eggs*

*Ruth Peek Neely. Goose, turkey, and duck eggs in simulated Fabergé style. One duck egg in decoupage. Used by permission.*

*Ruth Peek Neely. Vase made of a duck egg. Used by permission.*

# EGG HEADS AND EGG ANIMALS

Of all Easter eggs, few are more versatile than egg heads and their variation, egg animals. They all start out with a few basic steps, but after that, it is up to you. Practically anything can be used to decorate an egg head, and an egg head can represent practically anything. Even bits of copper pot scrubbers, odds and ends of yarn, cloth, paper, etc. may be used. If glue will hold it to an egg, it might come in handy in decorating an egg head.

## General Materials

Blown eggs—the color depends on what you plan to make

Egg dye in a background color if needed

Construction paper or other heavy paper

All-purpose white glue

## General Directions

1-If you plan to dye your egg flesh color (using a very light red) or a background color for an animal, do this first. Let the egg dry.

2-Cut a strip of construction paper about 1 inch wide and approximately 5 inches long, long enough to fit around the bottom of the egg with a slight overlap. This will form the base and is very like a link made for paper chains.

3-Glue the ends of the base together. Let dry.

4-Put a thin line of glue around the inside of the upper edge of the base. Fit the egg into the base and let it dry.

5-Decorate the egg head or egg animal any way you like. Or, use some of the suggestions which follow.

*Clown*

*From upper left: crazy quilt egg and crayon-etched egg (see page 147), and two batik-etched eggs, bleached and unbleached (see page 69)*

*Crayon-etched eggs*

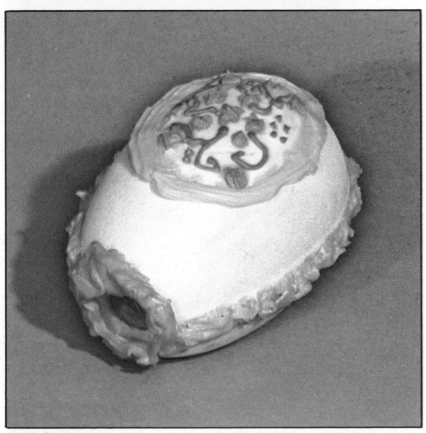

Peephole egg

# GRANDPA AND GRANDMA EGGS

This whimsical design has a slightly Victorian flavor.

*Materials*

> Blown white or brown eggs
> Pink egg dye if using white eggs
> Felt-tipped pens or watercolors for the features
> Construction paper for the bases
> All-purpose white glue
> White medical cotton
> Scraps of brightly colored felt, cloth, or paper, if Grandpa is to have a bow tie
> Scraps of lace or lace paper for Grandma's collar, if desired.

*Method*

1-Dye the blown eggs pale pink, or, use brown eggs and do not dye them. Allow the dyed eggs to dry well.
2-Make the bases as in General Directions on page 110. Glue the heads in place.
3-Paint on the facial features with the felt-tipped pens or with watercolors.
4-Make the hair by cutting strips from a roll of medical cotton. Glue on in layers for Grandma's topknot and in a circle for Grandpa's beard.
5-If desired, finish off the eggs with a jaunty bow tie for Grandpa and a lace collar for Grandma.

# HAWAIIAN HULA DANCER EGG HEAD

This exotic little lady will add zest to any celebration. And she's really quite easy to make.

## Materials

> Blown egg, dyed orange
> Construction paper strip 1 inch wide and 5 inches long for the base
> Green construction paper strip the same size as the base, for skirt
> Scraps of orange felt or fabric
> Gift wrapping ribbon, black or brown
> Tiny flowers cut from construction paper
> Black tempera paint
> All-purpose white glue

## Method

1-Make base and fasten egg in place as in General directions for egg heads and egg animals on page 110.
2-Clip the green construction paper strip to make fringe, making cuts ¾ inch deep and ⅛ inch to ¼ inch apart. Glue the skirt to the base.

3-Cut the arms and hands from the orange felt or fabric and glue in place as shown in diagram.
4-Make the hair by cutting 3-inch lengths of curling gift ribbon. Curl the ends by drawing ribbon between thumb and edge of scissors blade. Glue to the top of the head. Cut shorter lengths for the bangs and glue them in place.

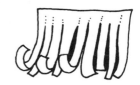

5-Cut tiny flowers from paper or fabric and glue them on for a lei effect. Make a slightly larger flower and glue in her hair.
6-Paint on two tiny black eyes and a black line for the mouth.

*Tiffany eggs*

*Eggshell candle*

# HIPPIE EGG HEAD

This is a timely egg head which will appeal to the older child or to the teen-ager who considers conventional eggs too babyish.

## Materials

A blown white or brown egg
Pink (very light red) egg dye if using a white egg
Construction paper strip for the base
Scraps of light red or brown construction paper for nose and ears
Scrap of colored construction paper for the eyes; or, use a marking pen
Scraps of felt for the hair
All-purpose white glue

## Method

1-If you are using a white egg, dye it a very light shade of red. If you are using a brown egg, skip this step.
2-Follow General Directions on page 110 for making the base.
3-Cut nose, ears, and eyes from construction paper and glue in place as shown.
4-Cut strips of felt for hair. These should be ⅛ inch wide and in varying lengths. Glue the end of each strip to the top of the egg to form the hair. Be just as shaggy as you like.
5-Repeat around the center of the egg for the beard.
6-Cut and glue a mustache.
7-After the glue is dry, if the hippie's hair and beard are too long give him a "trim."

# LIEUTENANT FLAP

Lieutenant Flap has quickly become a favorite in the "Beetle Bailey" comic strip. The basic method of making this character may also be used for many different black egg heads.

## Materials

Blown brown egg
Scraps of light brown construction paper and a 5-inch strip for a base
Scraps of khaki-colored construction paper
Scraps of black felt
Black yarn
All-purpose white glue
Felt-tipped pens or watercolors for marking the features

## Method

1-Following the General Directions on page 110, make the base and fasten the egg in it.
2-Cut ears and nose from light brown construction paper and glue in place as shown.
3-Cut black yarn in 1-inch to 1½-inch lengths and ravel out. Glue the raveled yarn to the top of the egg to form the Afro hair style. Make sideburns with shorter lengths of yarn.
4-Cut goatee and mustache from black felt and glue in place.
5-Mark facial features with felt-tipped pens or watercolors.
6-Cut Lieutenant Flap's collar from scraps of khaki-colored construction paper and glue in place.
7-Cut a necktie from scraps of black felt and glue in place.

*Traditional pysanky*

*Traditional pysanky. Photograph courtesy of National Museums of Canada.*

*Traditional pysanky. Photograph courtesy of National Museums of Canada.*

*Traditional pysanky. Photographs by Emil Basiuk,
courtesy of the Ukrainian Museum, Chicago.*

*Moon men and maidens.
Photograph courtesy the
National Cotton Council,
Memphis, Tennessee.*

## MOON MEN AND MOON MAIDENS

These are especially timely egg heads in our Space Age.

### Materials

Blown eggs
Construction paper
All-purpose white glue
Cotton swabs
Tempera paints
Scissors
Funnel if you plan to make a spacecraft

122

## Collage Eggs

*Method*

1-Make a base for each egg as directed on page 110 and fasten eggs into them.
2-Make a cut halfway along the shaft of a cotton swab to make antennae for each moon man or moon maiden. Do not cut all the way through. Bend on the cut to form a V. If desired, dip each tip into paint halfway. Let dry.
3-Glue the antenna in place on top of each egg. Hold in position until the glue dries. This will only take a few minutes.
4-Using a cotton swab or small paint brush, paint hair, helmets, facial features, and similar details on the eggs.
5-Cut ears from scraps of construction paper. Glue in place.
6-If you want to make a spacecraft, cut a window from dark paper and glue to the funnel. Cut a face for a moon man from lighter colored paper, paint on features, and glue to the window. Make the dots by dipping a swab into paint and pressing it against the funnel.

## EGG ANIMALS

Egg animals are a wonderful way to use your imagination. They don't need to be the least bit realistic, so if you want to turn out a purple lion—it will be perfect. The basic steps are the same as for egg heads, except that for many animals you will want to use a base which fits lengthwise on the eggshell. If you are going to paint an eggshell with tempera paint as the start of an egg animal, you might find it easier to handle if you run a thin knitting needle through both blowing holes in the egg and use the needle to hold the eggshell while you paint it. Tempera-painted eggshells may also be sprayed with plastic or acrylic spray to protect the paint if you wish.

*Easter bird*

*Egg mobile*

# EGG LION

The king of the beasts is always fun to make. Here he is a conventional lion, but you might want to make him a wild color for a change.

## Materials

    Blown egg—brown if you like
    Construction paper for the base, a 1-inch strip about 6
        inches long.
    Yellow-orange tempera paint
    Paintbrush
    Yellow or yellow-orange rug yarn
    Yellow or yellow-orange construction paper
    Felt-tipped pens or watercolors for marking the features
    All-purpose white glue

## Method

1-Paint the blown egg with tempera paint. Allow it to dry
    well.
2-Make the base to fit the egg lengthwise and glue in place
    (page 110).
3-Cut rug yarn into bits about 1 inch long and ravel them
    out. Glue the raveled yarn in place to form the lion's
    mane.
4-Cut a piece of rug yarn about 1 inch long and ravel out
    only at tip. Glue this in place to form his tail.
5-Cut ears from construction paper and glue in place.
6-Mark his features with the felt-tipped pens or watercolors.
    Or, cut them from scraps of construction paper and
    glue in place. (Do not try to use watercolors on the
    tempera-painted eggshell unless you have sprayed the
    shell first. They would just dissolve the tempera.)

CAUTION

126

# MR. RABBIT

Mr. Rabbit is a bit different from most egg animal bunnies. He will appeal to older children who consider rabbits strictly for the kindergarten set.

## Materials

> Blown eggs colored any wacky shade you like
> Three large sequins
> Two pipe cleaners
> Construction paper for whiskers and eyebrows
> Two small cotton powder puffs
> Small ribbon bow
> Small artificial flowers
> Curtain ring
> All-purpose white glue

## Method

1-Cut ears from one powder puff. Glue a pipe cleaner, dyed if you like, lengthwise down the center of each ear.
2-Carefully prick two small holes in the eggshell where you want the ears to go. Glue ears in place with the ends of the pipe cleaners resting in the holes.
3-Cut whiskers and eyebrows from construction paper. Glue in place. Glue sequin eyes and mouth in place over eyebrows and whiskers.
4-Glue Mr. Rabbit to the curtain ring and use the other powder puff as a base.

127

*Easter egg tree*

## EASTER EGG PIGS

Most preschoolers love Easter egg pigs. They are fun to make and attractive to busy mothers who dislike the mess so often associated with Easter eggs. With mother to handle the knife, Easter egg pigs can be made by most four-year-olds.

*Suitable for very young children*

### Materials

Hardcooked, white egg for each pig
5 small gumdrops for each pig. Be sure to use fresh gumdrops; stale ones won't stick properly.
Sharp knife

### Method

1-Cut a thin slice from the flat end of each gumdrop. Save
   the cut-off bits.
2-Press 4 of the gumdrops in place to form the pig's legs.
3-Cut the fifth gumdrop in half lengthwise. Use the gumdrop halves for the pig's ears.
4-Cut eyes, nose, and tail from the saved bits of gumdrop.
   Press in place.

*From top, clockwise: peephole egg, crayon-etched egg, three Tiffany eggs, a second crayon-etched egg, and, in center, finger-painted egg.*

# MiSCELLANEOUS EGGS

## MADRAS EGGS

Madras eggs are reminiscent of calico eggs which were popular in the United States in the early 1800s. It would be hard to make real calico eggs today because almost all cloth is colorfast. You will get good results with scraps of bleeding madras.

### Materials

> Blown white eggs or raw white eggs too stale to be used
>    for food
> For each egg, a scrap of madras at least 6 inches square
> String

### Method

1-Wrap the madras around each egg. Tie it in place with
    string.
2-Boil the eggs in their madras dresses. If you use blown eggs,
    you will have to keep pushing them under the water.
3-When the eggs have cooled enough to handle, unwrap
    them. You will have the outlines of the lines of the
    madras on your egg.

These eggs are not a food item.                          *CAUTION*

# FINGER-PAINTED EGGS

CAUTION

Older children or adults might like to try decorating Easter eggs with finger paints. Since the wet eggs are exceedingly slippery, this is not a project for young ones.

## Materials

Hardcooked, or blown white eggs
Finger paints—commercial or made from the recipe given below

## Method

1-Do one half of each egg at a time. Coat the surface with finger paint and work out your own design as you go.
2-Let dry and then repeat on the other half of the egg.

## Finger Paint

If you want to try finger-painted eggs and do not have any paint, make your own this way:
Combine:
¼ cup laundry starch
Small amount of cold water
1 pint boiling water
¼ cup mild soapflakes
2 tablespoons inexpensive talcum powder, if desired
Poster paint
Small jars, 1 for each color

Soften the starch in a small amount of cold water. Gradually add the pint of boiling water to the starch mixture. Make a thick starch mixture, stirring until it bubbles up. Remove from the heat and let cool a bit. Add the soapflakes and talcum, if desired. Divide mixture into several small jars. Baby food jars are ideal for this quantity of paint. Add a different color poster paint to each jar of starch mixture. Either dry or liquid poster paint may be used.

*Finger-painted egg*

## COMIC STRIP EGGS—TRANSFER METHOD

Even if you don't have as much as an onion skin in the house, you can make these novel Easter eggs. They require no dye at all.

### Materials

Colored comic pages—the inkier the better
White candle or a block of white wax
Hardcooked white eggs
Spoon or tongue depressor

*Method*

1-Choose good, heavily inked comic strip pages; older pages
  on which the ink is very dry will not work as well.
2-Have the eggs at room temperature or very slightly warm
  for best results.
3-Cut out a figure from the comic pages. Be sure it will fit
  on the egg.
4-Rub the surface of the egg well with the candle or block
  of wax. Do this where you want your comic strip transfer.
5-Place the cut-out, right side down, on the wax coated egg.
  Rub the back of the cut-out with the spoon or tongue
  depressor, taking care to rub the entire surface. The
  colored design will transfer to the egg.

## PEEPHOLE EASTER EGGS

For many older people, memories of childhood Easters
center on the beautiful peephole eggs which were so much
a part of holiday fun in the late nineteenth and early twen-
tieth centuries. Even today's sophisticated children find the
old-world charm of these eggs irresistible. Sparkling white
sugar forms the shell; a tiny window at one end admits the
viewer to a land of enchantment within. Whether an intricate
panorama or merely a prosiac bunny hiding his colored eggs
for the children to find on Easter morning are seen inside, the
imagination knows no bounds. The Space Age, for all its
excitement, still produces nothing quite like the magic of a
peephole Easter egg.

## Miscellaneous Eggs

Though these lovely eggs require time and patience to make, anyone who is willing to work slowly and carefully can produce a very attractive one on the first attempt. Anyone who has already mastered cake decorating techniques will find them quite simple to do. With a little practice, their creator will have a highly popular bazaar item and, after friends have seen the work, there may be more orders than can be filled. Fortunately, the materials needed to make peephole eggs are neither hard to find nor expensive.

Crystal sugar makes the most handsome eggs. If you live near a cake-decorating supply house and can get this specialty item, use it for your eggs; otherwise, make them from regular granulated sugar. Most people do. Quantities given apply to either type of sugar.

Peephole egg molds are made from plastic and may have either one or two sections. Most molds are two-piece affairs, shaped like an egg, and divided in half lengthwise. The best ones have a flattened place, or foot, on the bottom half. The foot keeps the  finished egg from rolling, if it is displayed on a table. Molds may be found in hobby shops, stores specializing in party supplies, and in variety stores, where they are sold as containers for Easter treats. In some areas, they may be known as panoramic egg molds. You will need only one two-piece mold for each size of egg you plan to make, since the egg-halves are shaped in the molds and then turned out to dry. If necessary, you could get by with a half-egg mold. Depending on size and type, they usually cost from ten cents to about one dollar each.

Measurements and drying times are intended as guidelines only. Because egg whites vary so much in size, and because temperature and humidity can greatly affect the rate at which the sugar and egg-white mixture dries, it is impossible to give exact figures. When the mixture behaves as described in the directions, the consistency is right. When the molded halves reach the specified degree of hardness, it is time to go on to the next step—regardless of what the clock says.

# Easter Eggs For Everyone

*Materials*

Two-piece, or single-sided, plastic egg molds in sizes you wish to make. Though molds vary greatly in size, a large mold generally holds about 2 cups of liquid in each half; a small one holds approximately 1/3 cup in each half.

Cardboard—a medium weight sheet at least 6 inches square

Cardboard—a 3-inch square for each egg if your mold does not have a foot

Breadboard, tabletop, or other smooth, solid surface for drying the eggs.

Aluminum foil or plastic wrap—a sheet large enough to cover the breadboard or other drying surface

Sharp paring knife

Teaspoon

Scissors

Celluloid—a window from a wallet-sized cardholder is ideal. You will need one for each large egg, or, half of one for each small egg.

Cake decorating set or pastry tube

Food coloring, either liquid or paste

Large mixing bowl

Cups or small bowls for coloring icing

Tiny figures and/or scenery for the panorama

Sugars, crystal or granulated, and confectioners', in the amounts specified in the recipes below

Egg whites, in the amount specified in the recipes below

Cream of tartar for icing

Cornstarch

In making a large egg and a small one, the large egg is made first, and the small one is made from sugar hollowed out of the larger egg after it has undergone the first drying out. You do not make both eggs at the same time.

*Method*

## Sugar Eggshells for Peephole Eggs

(The preparation and handling of the sugar and egg-white mixture is the same no matter how many eggs you are making, only the proportions of the ingredients change.)

*For 1 large egg and one small egg, or, for 2 small eggs:*
    3 1/3 to 4 cups sugar, crystal or granulated
    1 medium egg white

*For 4 large eggs, or, 8 small eggs:*
    5 pounds sugar, crystal or granulated
    3 medium egg whites

If you have never made peephole eggs before, be sure to start out with the smaller quantities.

1-Prepare a place where the molded egg sections may dry undisturbed. This could be a foil- or plastic-covered breadboard, tabletop, or some other place where the eggs will be exposed to the air, but will not be bumped or moved about. Do not cover the drying surface with cloth; the sugar and egg-white mixture will stick to it. Do not dry the eggs in a cabinet or other closed place. They need circulating air in order to dry properly.

2-Using the quantities given for the number of eggs you plan to make and starting with the smallest amount of sugar, combine the sugar and unbeaten egg whites in a large bowl. Mix well. If you want colored eggshells, add food coloring a little at a time until you get the desired shade.

3-Put about 1 teaspoon of cornstarch into one half of an egg mold and shake until the inside is evenly coated with starch. Shake out the excess starch.

4-To test the sugar mixture for consistency, press some of it into one half of the coated mold. Fill so that the sugar mixture rounds up slightly above the open side of the mold as shown. Using a clean sheet of cardboard, press

hard against the mixture until the sugar is flattened out and solidly packed in the mold. If a slight hollow develops on the surface, after you have pressed it down, add a little more sugar and egg mixture and press down again.

Holding the cardboard firmly against the flattened surface of the sugar, invert the egg onto the drying surface as shown and slip the cardboard from underneath. Lift off plastic egg mold. Look at the inside of the mold. If crumbs of sugar and egg-white mixture appear on the inside of the mold, return the trial egg-half to the bowl and gradually add additional sugar, about ¼ cup at a time.

Wipe out the inside of the mold, dust with cornstarch again, and retest. The egg-half should come out of the mold smoothly, leaving no crumbs behind and holding together well when it is unmolded.

If the sugar mixture fails to hold together smoothly, return the test half to the bowl and add a few additional drops of egg white. Repeat the test after cleaning the mold and dusting it again with cornstarch.

5-When the sugar mixture molds as it should, form the rest of your egg halves, following the same directions for molding the test egg halves. Leave a few inches between each half on the drying surface. If you have never made a peephole egg before, you might like to mold an extra half, if you have enough sugar and egg-white mixture. The halves are very fragile in the early stages.

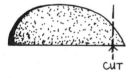

CUT

6-Before the egg-halves begin to dry, cut a ½-inch slice from the narrow end of each molded half for a large egg. Cut a ¼-inch slice from each narrow end for the small eggs.

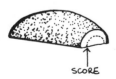

SCORE

7-Using the point of a knife, carefully score around the cut end of each egg-half. The scoring should be done ⅜ inch from the outer crust and ¼ inch deep on the large eggs. For the small eggs, score ¼ inch from the outer crust surface and make the cut ¼ inch deep. At a later time, the inner core of this scored section will be removed to form the window in the egg. When this scoring is done before the egg begins to dry, the egg-half is less likely to break when the window is made. (At this point the egg-halves shatter very easily.)

8-Allow the small egg-halves to dry for about 1 hour. The large halves should dry for about 3 hours. At the end of the drying time, carefully pick up one of the halves and turn it flat-side up, holding the rounded side in your hand. Starting at the outer edge, test gently with your fingernail along the rim of flattened surface. The outer crust should be dry and hard, and by testing with your fingernail you can determine how thick the hardened crust is.

The finished thickness of the shell on a large egg should be ½ inch thick, and the finished thickness of a small egg should be ¼ inch thick. For both sizes of eggs, the thickness of the shells should taper to ¼ inch at the window-opening.

If the shell has reached the proper thickness, go on to the next step. If the outer shell is too thin, carefully replace the egg, flat-side down, on the drying surface and allow the halves to harden a little longer. If the weather is especially humid, the drying time will be somewhat longer. Do not go on to step 9 until the outer shell is the correct thickness.

9-When the outer shell on the small eggs is ¼ inch thick and the outer shell on the large eggs is ½ inch thick, the egg halves should be hollowed out. Pick up each egg-half and turn it flat-side up in your hand. Using the tip of a teaspoon as a scoop gently remove the inner core of the scored section. Removing the window first will reduce the danger of breaking the fragile shells. Then carefully scoop out the sugar and egg-white mixture which is still soft in the center of the egg. When the tip of your spoon hits the hard outer shell, you have

139

gone deep enough. Put the scooped-out sugar in a small bowl and cover it with plastic or foil until you are ready to use it.

10-Put the hollowed-out egg-halves, flat-side down, on the drying surface and allow to dry for at least another hour before going on to step 11.

While the hollowed-out egg-halves are drying, you may mold other halves with the scooped-out sugar and egg-white mixture, or it may be stored, tightly covered, in the refrigerator for several days. If you do not plan to reuse the mixture, spread it on a cookie sheet, allow to dry well, then crush. Use for household purposes such as sprinkling on cookies.

11-Make the Royal Icing

### Royal Icing

(This quantity of icing will do *1 large egg, or, 2 small eggs. Double the recipe if you are making 2 large eggs and 1 small one.*)

    1 medium egg white
    ⅛ teaspoon cream of tartar
    1¾ cups sifted confectioners' sugar

For *4 large eggs, or, 8 small ones:*

    3 medium egg whites
    ¼ teaspoon cream of tartar
    6 cups sifted confectioners' sugar

Place the egg whites in a bowl with the cream of tartar. Beat until foamy. Gradually beat in the confectioners' sugar, until the mixture is stiff enough to hold a sharp line when cut through with a knife. Divide the icing into smaller portions for coloring. Color one part to use for the ground (green for grass, brown for earth, blue for sea), and the remaining portions, whatever colors you like for decorating the egg. Royal icing will keep for several days if it is stored in an airtight *glass* container, a jar with a screw-on top is ideal, and kept in the refrigerator. Do not store in a plastic container. Plastic causes this icing to break down. Never leave the icing uncovered; it will become rock-hard in a very short time.  *CAUTION*

12-When your egg-halves are dry, make a foot for each bottom half if your mold does not have a flat base. Cut a circle or oval about 1 inch in diameter from scrap cardboard. Glue this with icing to the bottom of the egg. Using a pastry tube and a decorative tip, pipe additional icing around the edge of the cardboard, covering it completely. If you like, the surface of the cardboard may also be iced. Allow the egg to dry for several hours.

13-Plan your scene. This may be as simple or as elaborate as you like, but keep it small. You may make your own figures, or find suitable ones around the house, or buy them in a hobby shop.

14-(If your molds have a foot, and you are not waiting for the base to dry, go right on to this step:)

Put a layer of icing in the bottom half of each egg to represent the ground or sea or whatever. Make it deep enough to hold your scene in place, but do not overdo it. While the icing is wet, arrange the scene in the bottom of the egg, anchoring it in the icing. Place the figures so that an attractive panorama is formed, but be careful that the objects do not block one another from view when you look into the egg. Allow the scene to dry well before assembling the egg.

15-If desired, the inside top half of each egg may be covered with blue icing to form a sky. Start this color at the point where your vision begins as you look through the peephole. If the entire top of the egg is lined with icing, the light needed to see the scene will be blocked out. Allow to dry well.

16-Using icing as glue, put the halves together. If you made a sky, use blue icing for the glue; the blue from the top tends to bleed a bit and will discolor other colors. Remove excess icing-glue from the outside of the egg. Allow the egg to dry ½ hour.

17-Now you are ready to put the window in place. With a pastry tube and plain tip, pipe a ring of icing around the edge of the window opening. Press the uncut celluloid against the wet icing. Remove immediately and trim along the icing outline. Press the window in place. With a decorative tip on the pastry tube, outline the window. Cover the seam in the egg where the two sides are put together with the same border. Allow the icing to dry before decorating the top of the egg.

18-Decorate the top of the egg with flowers, leaves, etc. Now stand back and admire your own handiwork. Allow to dry again before handling the finished egg.

## Variations

Make the peephole at the side of the egg rather than on the end. Or, you may prefer to leave small eggs whole, omitting the peephole and the scene.

142

# PEEPHOLE EASTER EGGS AND THE
# SPECIAL CHILD

By varying the technique a bit, mentally retarded or spastic children can make attractive peephole Easter eggs. They will need a bit of help from a person with normal finger control, but they'll love doing the eggs. In this method, the eggs are not made of sugar, rather the plastic molds themselves are decorated to make the peephole egg.

*Also suitable for the young child*

## Materials

Two-piece plastic egg molds
Clear plastic for the windows
All-purpose white glue
Florists' clay
Tiny figures for the scenery
Lace, beads, flowers, or whatever can be glued on to decorate the outside of the egg
An X-Acto knife or similar tool
Curtain rings, if desired

## Method

1-Have an older person with normal finger control cut the window in each plastic egg mold.
2-Put a layer of florist's clay in the bottom of the lower half of the mold.
3-Arrange the scenery in the florists' clay.
4-Glue the 2 halves of the mold together.
5-Glue the window in place.
6-Decorate the outside of the egg with lace, beads, etc.
7-If desired, glue a curtain ring to the bottom of the egg to serve as a foot.

# TIFFANY EGGS GLACE

These novel "for show" eggs prove that literally anything can be used to decorate Easter eggs. Since the eggshells are completely covered up, brown eggs may be used if you wish.

## Materials

Blown eggs
Cake decorating tube with a plain tip—preferably metal
   1 package spackling compound in powder form. This compound is similar to plaster of paris and is used to fill cracks or other blemishes in many types of surfaces, including plaster and metal. It may be bought at most paint and hardware stores. Spackling compound is often sold in one pound packages.
Paper toweling
Large plastic dish
Poster paint in a variety of bright colors
Paint brushes
Clear varnish
Small paper cups or eggcups

## Method

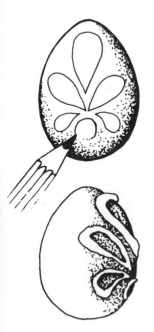

1-In the plastic dish mix about 1 cup of the spackling compound with cold water until it is smooth and thin enough to flow evenly from a cake decorating tube with a plain tip.
2-Lightly pencil a simple, bold design on your eggshell.
3-Using the decorating tube, apply the spackle to the design outline on one half of the egg only. Wipe the tip frequently with paper toweling to prevent dripping spackle.
4-Set the egg aside in one of the paper cups or in an eggcup. Allow it to dry for several hours or overnight.

5-When you have completed as many egg halves as you wish, immediately wash and dry all utensils before spackling compound hardens in them.

6-Repeat steps 1, 3, 4, and 5 with the other half of each egg. A knitting needle run through the blowing holes makes it easy to hold the eggs when decorating the other halves. They are extremely fragile at this point.

7-After both sides of the egg have dried thoroughly, mix your poster paint if you are using powdered colors. If you are using premixed paint, thin it slightly with water. Paint that is too thick will cause the spackle to crack.

8-Paint the recessed surfaces of the eggshell first, then the raised spackled design. Do one half of the egg at a time. Let each half dry before doing the other. Again, use the knitting needle as handle.

9-When the paint is dry, apply varnish to the first half, let it dry, then varnish the other half.

145

# CRAYON-ETCHED EGGS

Crayon-etched eggs can be whatever you want them to be. They are suitable for use with children old enough to avoid pressing too hard on the eggshells when applying the crayon. The more sophisticated version, tweed eggs, will appeal to older egg crafters.

## Materials

Hardcooked eggs, dry and at room temperature
Wax crayons in any combination of colors you like; one should be black
Sharp-pointed tools for scratching out the design— knife, needle, etc.

## Method

1-Be sure the egg is dry and at room temperature. An egg which is damp, cold, or more than slightly warm will not take the wax crayon properly.
2-Cover the entire surface of the egg with heavy coat of the lightest color wax crayon.
3-Repeat with one or more colors. Put the additional layers of crayon on top of the earlier ones. For best results, make the top layer black. Two colors plus black works very well.
4-Using the sharp instrument, scratch out any design you like. Cut through all the layers of crayon or through only one or two layers.
5-For variety, use several scratching tools with points of different widths.

# CRAZY-QUILT EGGS

Crazy-quilt eggs are a more sophisticated version of crayon-etched eggs.

## *Materials*

Use exactly the same materials as for crayon-etched eggs.

## *Method*

1-Apply the crayon in random splotches of different colors over the surface of the egg.
2-Build up three or four layers of crayon, making each one different. Use two or three colors in each layer. Make the last layer black.
3-Scratch out your patchwork design as for crayon-etched eggs.

# TWEED EGGS

Tweed eggs are very pretty and extremely easy to do.

## Materials

Hardcooked eggs, dry and at room temperature
Crayons in 2 pastel colors.
Black crayon
Knife with a fairly sharp blade.

## Method

1-Cover the entire surface of the egg with the lightest color crayon, using long strokes that go from end to end on the egg.
2-Repeat with the second color crayon, again going from end to end on the egg.
3-Apply a layer of black crayon.
4-Using the blade of the knife and working from end to end, gently scrape the entire surface of the egg to remove the crayon. Since eggs are slightly rough, the crayon will remain in tiny hollows. You will have a tweedy looking egg in black, white, and two colors.

148

# STYROFOAM EGGS

Styrofoam eggs are another boon for those working with handicapped children. They may be decorated by gluing on anything the child desires, or, by painting them. Or, felt slipcovers may be sewed on the eggs.

Styrofoam eggs may also be decorated in the same manner as similar ornaments used at Christmas.

Trimmings made from bright cloth or ribbon and often ornaments fashioned from beads or sequins are fastened to the eggs with straight pins. Or they may be glued in place.

For a novel variation sew a felt slipcover for the egg. Decorate it with embroidered or glued-on flowers, and use as a pin cushion.

For use in libraries or other places where Easter eggs form an annual part of the decorations, styrofoam eggs may be painted with tempera paint. Rather large designs are usually best for this. The eggs are sturdy and are easily stored from year to year.

*Suitable for use with the very young and also with the special child*

149

# EASTER EGG NOVELTIES

## CONFETTI EGGS

Confetti eggs are a pretty addition to an Easter party. They sound complicated but are easy and fun to make.

### Materials

Blown white eggs, colored or decorated as you like
Confetti (available in the party section of a variety store)
Scraps of paper
All-purpose white glue or rubber cement.

### Method

1-When you blow your eggs, make the hole in one end a bit larger than usual. Do this very carefully with an ice pick or skewer. Dry the shells well before going on to step 2.
2-Make a small funnel from a rolled piece of paper.
3-Use the funnel to help you fill the eggshells with the confetti
4-Glue a tiny piece of paper over the hole. When the glue has dried, tear away the excess paper. Or, cover the hole with a bit of transparent tape.

150

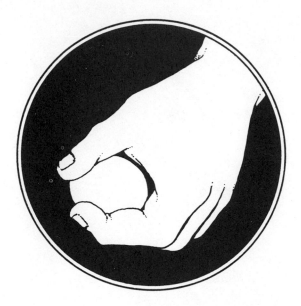

To use a confetti egg in a magic trick, hold the egg in your right hand and show it to the audience. Close your hand and wave it in the air. As you close your hand, hold your thumb over one hole and your fingers over the other. The gentle pressure will crush the shell, and the confetti will be released. The bits of shell will fall unnoticed with thc confetti.

## EASTER-BIRDS

An unusual type of Easter egg was popular in the Pennsylvania Dutch country about one hundred years ago. This was the *Ochter-foggel*, or Easter-bird. The birds were of German origin and were made from blown, colored eggs. They had wings and a tail made of pleated paper and a string for hanging was fastened in a hole in the bird's back. A few of the original birds still exist and are highly prized by their owners.

The Easter-birds might be called the forerunners of today's Easter mobiles.

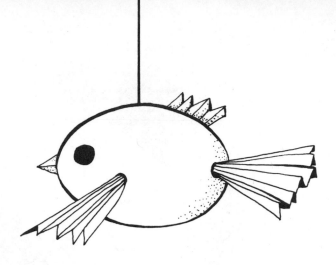

## Materials

Blown, dyed egg for each bird
3 pieces of thin, brightly colored paper for each bird.
  Pieces should be about 2¾ inches by 8 inches.
Small scrap of yellow construction paper for the beak
Ice pick or skewer
All-purpose white glue
Thin string for hanging

## Method

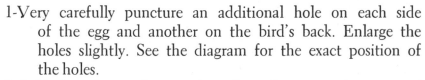

1-Very carefully puncture an additional hole on each side
  of the egg and another on the bird's back. Enlarge the
  holes slightly. See the diagram for the exact position of
  the holes.
2-Fold the pieces of paper into fine pleats, running up and
  down the 2¾ inch side. Hold the paper tightly pleated
  together.
3-Carefully insert one end of the folded wing and tail pieces
  into place, putting a wing in each of the side holes and
  the tail in the rear blowing hole.
4-Cut a beak from the construction paper and glue in place.
5-If desired, mark eyes with a felt-tipped pen or crayon.
6-Tie a small knot in one end of the string and gently work
  the knot through the top hole. Hang the completed
  birds.

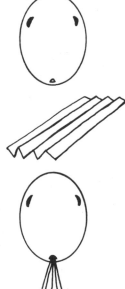

152

## EASTER EGG CANDLES

Easter egg candles make a pleasant addition to almost any Easter table. They may be purchased in some specialty shops, but are usually quite expensive. With a few materials found in most homes and a little time, you can make your own successfully. Easter egg candles are a good craft project for any one who is able to work safely with melted wax.

153

# Easter Eggs For Everyone

*Materials*

Blown eggs with membrane left in. The shells must be thoroughly dry.

Fine white twine

Scraps of pastel wax crayon. Allow ½ crayon to each pint of melted wax.

Paraffin (wax), bits of old candles, or a mixture of both

A few pieces of uncooked spaghetti, or a pencil (stub) for each egg.

Large pot and large tin can for melting wax

Empty egg carton

Old spoon or stick for stirring wax

Small funnel for pouring wax. This can be made from waxed paper or cardboard

Newspapers

Construction paper for drying bases

Oil paints or tiny decals, if desired

Coarse sandpaper, if desired

*Method*

1-Melt the paraffin (wax) in the tin can set in an inch or two of boiling water in the large pot.

2-When the wax has completely melted, add the bits of crayon and stir until they are well mixed.

3-Remove from the heat, but keep over hot water while you work. If the wax should begin to harden, reheat.

4-To make the wicks, cut the string into 10-inch pieces. Then twist 2 pieces of string together to form 1 wick. Dip the wicks into the melted wax and crayon mixture. Stretch on several thicknesses of newspaper to dry. When the wicks are cool enough to handle, fold each one in half and twist tightly. You will have wicks 5 inches long.

5-Slightly enlarge the hole in the small end of the egg enough for the wick to slip through. Enlarge the hole in the large end of the egg until it is about the size of a five-cent piece.

6-Thread the wick through the eggshell, leaving about ⅜ inch of the wick extending outside the small hole. At the large end, twist the extra length of wick around a pencil or piece of spaghetti laid across the opening in the bottom of the egg. Pull the wick inside the egg straight.

7-Put the eggshells, small-end down, in compartments in the egg carton. Using small funnel, carefully fill each eggshell with the melted wax mixture. The wax will shrink slightly as it dries. Add more melted wax until the wax is about level with the opening in the large end of the egg.

8-Remove the filled eggshells from the carton and place in cups or similar container lined with plastic wrap. Allow the wax to harden well. (If you leave the filled shells in the carton through the whole process, the leaking wax will glue the eggshells so firmly to the container that it will be very difficult to remove them.)

9-Roll each egg on a table or other hard surface to crack the shells. Peel off the shell, trim the bottom of each candle so that it is flat, or, smooth the bottoms of the candles by rubbing them on coarse sandpaper. Decorate the finished candles with oil paints or small decals, if desired.

# EGG MOBILES

Egg mobiles make fascinating year-round decorations. The balancing is a bit tricky but beyond that, they're pure fun to make.

## Materials

> Several old wire clothes hangers, or about 3 feet of galvanized wire
> Long-nosed pliers
> Nylon thread, or fishing line
> A few wooden matches
> Blown, decorated eggs

## Method

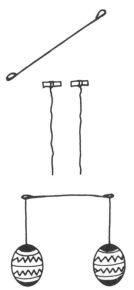

1-Use the long-nosed pliers to cut the wire into lengths. Have the first one about 4 inches long, the next about 6 inches long, the next about 8 inches and the fourth about 10 inches. You may use more lengths of wire if you like, but 4 is usually enough for a start.

2-Using the pliers, make a small loop at each end of the lengths of wire, which will be the arms of the mobile.

3-Break the matches into short bits. Tie a piece of nylon thread or fishing line to the center of each piece of matchstick. The length of the strings should be a little less than the distance between the wire arms is to be. Fix one piece for each egg you plan to use in the mobile.

4-Slip one of the pieces of matchstick through the blowing hole in the top of each eggshell. Leave the string hanging out. The piece of matchstick will wedge itself crosswise inside the egg and allow you to hang the shells on the arms.

5-Beginning with the shortest arm, tie a decorated egg to the loops at each end.

156

6-Find the balancing point on the short arm. Cut a piece of the nylon thread or fishing line the length of the distance desired between this arm and the next one. Tie one end to the first arm at the balancing point; then tie the other end to the next shortest arm.

7-Make the other arms of the mobile in the same way, working from the shortest to the longest.

8-Hang your mobile.

## EGGSHELL MOSAICS

Eggshell mosaics make an excellent Easter craft project for school or Scouts. They may be used to make pictures or designs on a piece of cardboard, or, used to decorate the outsides of boxes or jars to make handsome gifts. The best part of making eggshell mosaics is that the main material is found in any home. If the mosaics are being made as a school project, have each child prepare and dye his own eggshells at home. And do allow sufficient work time, for even a very simple mosaic can take an hour or more.

# Easter Egg Novelties

## *Materials*

> Empty eggshells—broken ones are fine, but allow the equivalent of at least 8 whole eggshells for each mosaic (8½ inches by 11 inches in size).
> Empty egg cartons for storing the dyed shells
> Egg dye
> Tweezers or a pencil with an eraser on the end or both
> Paper clip, straightened out
> Pencil
> Sheet of cardboard, 8½ inches by 11 inches, or any size you want for your mosaic, or, paper to fit around the jar or box you plan to use and a piece of paper the size of the jar or box lid
> Shellac, if desired
> Paint brushes, if desired

## *Method*

1-Begin to collect empty eggshells well ahead of time. Rinse the shells as you get them, let them dry well, and store them until you have enough to dye.

2-Remove as much of the inner membrane as possible; the membrane makes it harder to handle the dyed eggshells.

3-Draw the outlines of a simple picture or design on a piece of cardboard, or, on the piece of paper you plan to use to cover your box or jar.

4-Dye the broken eggshells any colors you plan to use in your mosaics. Spread on paper to dry well, then store them, sorted by color and size, in the empty egg cartons.

5-Break the eggshells into small pieces, ranging from ⅛ inch to 1 inch in size. Keep all pieces of one color together.

6-If you are doing a box or jar, glue the paper in place next.

7-Starting at the outer edge of the design, apply paste or all-purpose glue to a small part of the area at a time. Using the tweezers and the paper clip to help you, put your bits of dyed eggshell in place on the glue-covered parts of your pattern. Or, use the eraser end of a pencil dipped in a tiny bit of paste to help you pick up the pieces of eggshell. As you get each bit in place, use the eraser end of a clean pencil or your finger to press down on the larger pieces of shell, breaking them into finer bits. Use tiny pieces of shell to fill in the spaces. Keep on applying glue or paste to a small part of the design at a time and filling it in with dyed eggshell bits, until you have the whole design covered. This will take time and patience.

8-If desired, coat the finished mosaics with shellac.

## EGGSHELL VASES

These miniature vases are just the right size to hold tiny bouquets or a single rosebud. Or, you might want to plant a short-stemmed flower in one for a special Easter gift.

*Materials*

Eggs
Darning needle
Quick-drying hobby enamels
Paint brushes
Construction paper
All-purpose white glue
Toothpicks

160

## Method

1-Empty the eggshells by making a small hole in the narrow end of each one with a darning needle. Use the needle to break away the shell a little at a time until the opening measures about ¾ inch across. Turn the egg upside down over a bowl and shake out the white and the yolk. Use them in cooking. Blown eggs are not used because a solid bottom is needed to hold the water for the flowers.

2-Rinse out the eggshells and turn them upside down to dry.

3-When the inside is dry, paint the outside of the shells with hobby enamel. Leave them just one color, or, decorate the vases by painting a design on one side.

4-Make the base from matching or contrasting colored construction paper. Draw a circle 2 inches in diameter. Inside it draw another circle 1½ inches in diameter. Mark

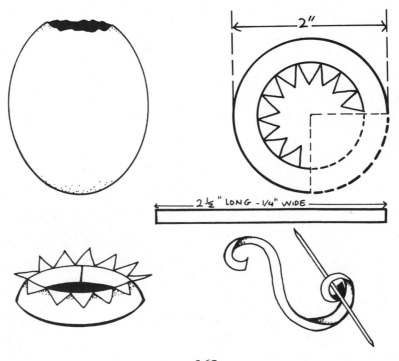

off ¼ of the circle and inside the rest draw points as shown. Cut around the remaining ¾ of the circle and the points. Lap and glue the ends together and fold the points outward as shown. Spread glue on the insides of the points and set the eggshell, cut side up, on the base. Press the points against the shell.

5-Make the handles by cutting 2 strips of construction paper each ¼ inch wide and 2½ inches long. Roll the ends around a toothpick and shape the handles as shown.

6-Glue the handles to the sides of the vase as shown.

7-If you want a vase with a single handle, cut a strip ¼ inch wide and 9 inches long. Glue the ends to the base points at opposite sides of the shell with the handle curving over the top as shown.

8-Partly fill the vase with water and arrange your bouquet. Or, fill it with soil and plant a small flower in the eggshell vase.

# EASTER EGG TREES

Easter egg trees make excellent craft projects for school or Scouts. Even preschoolers can make them very successfully, if they have a bit of supervision. The trees make lovely holiday decorations for schools or other institutions. Many libraries feature Easter egg trees in the children's department each year. An egg tree may also be used at home—a large one on the floor or a miniature one as a centerpiece at Easter dinner.

## Materials for an Indoor Egg Tree

>  Bushy tree branch of the desired size
>  Empty tin can or other container of the proper size for the base.
>  The size will depend on the size of the branch.
>  Plaster of paris, plasticene, or florists' clay. Get enough to hold the branch securely in the can.
>  White paint, whitewash, or metallic paint, if desired. The paint may be either regular or spray. Spray paint is easier to handle.
>  Paint brushes
>  Blown white eggs
>  Egg dye
>  Narrow ribbon—get a piece 5 inches long for each egg.
>  All-purpose white glue
>  Other decorations if desired. You might want to add Easter cookies with a loop for hanging, artificial flowers, or candy.

## Method

1-The branch may be used in its natural state. Or, spray or brush the branch with paint or whitewash. Allow it to dry.
2-If desired, paint the tin can or cover it with paper or foil.

3-Half fill the can with plaster of paris, mixed with water until it is quite thick.

4-Anchor the branch firmly in the wet plaster. Add more plaster if necessary. Keep the branch steady until the plaster has set. Or, hold it in place with a layer of plasticene or florists' clay.

5-Blow and decorate the eggs. Using the liquid white glue. attach a loop of ribbon to one end of each egg. Allow the glue to dry before hanging the eggs on the tree. Or, run a looped strand of heavy thread through the holes in the egg. Leave a loop at one end for hanging. Fasten the thread, preferably at the small end, by running it through a tiny button.

6-Decorate the tree with the colored eggs and also with cookies, candy, or flowers, if you choose.

## EGG TREES FOR KINDERGARTNERS

Kindergarten children dearly love Easter egg trees. With some advance preparation, an egg tree makes an exciting school project for children this age.

Several days ahead of time, perhaps using a branch supplied by one of the children, the teacher prepares the tree and brings it to class. On the big day, have each child bring at least 2 raw eggs to school. After the teacher marks each child's initials on his eggs, she punctures the eggs. Then the children, with any needed help from her, blow their own.

Depending on the amount of time and adult assistance available, have an egg-dyeing party for the children either that day or the following day (see pages 167-70). Have the children decorate the dyed eggs with crayons. Gently work one end of a pipe cleaner about 1 inch into the top hole in the egg. Bend the pipe cleaner to form a hanger. Have each child hang his own eggs on the class tree. After Easter, the children get their own eggs to take home.

# EASTER ENTERTAINMENTS

## AN EGG-DYEING PARTY

Egg-dyeing parties don't have to send the grown--up-in-charge to a tranquilizer bottle after the last guest has gone home, if the advance planning has been careful and thorough. With some forethought, egg-dyeing parties can be successfully conducted for any age group, including pre-schoolers.

As with any other party, the age and sex of the children must be considered when preparing the guest list. Small children do well in mixed groups but slightly older ones are better off with all-girl or all-boy parties. Don't invite more guests than you can handle easily with the number of adults available. If at all possible, get a neighbor in to help for the afternoon.

As soon as you decide to have the party, begin to save old newspapers. You'll need plenty. If the party is a spur-of-the-moment one, beg extras from your friends. The more newspapers you have on hand, the less likely you are to have damage done to your furniture and flooring.

An extra roll or two of paper towels is another must. And decide what you want to use for dye containers. Discarded one-pound size unwaxed cottage cheese cartons are excellent for use with small children. They are large enough to handle comfortably and do not tip over easily. Well-washed and cut-down plastic bleach bottles (one quart size) are also good. So are styrofoam hot-and-cold cups. They're inexpensive to buy and can be thrown out after the party is over. But don't use styrofoam cups with children in the spilling stage; they're more tippable than the other possibilities.

CAUTION    Check your supply of vinegar several days ahead of time. For an egg dyeing party, you ought to have at least a cupful on hand. While you're at it, be sure you have enough egg dippers or tablespoons on hand for each guest to have one. Unless you are planning to do striped eggs, the children will do as well with spoons.

Lay in a good supply of egg-decorating items if you plan to carry the party that far. Very small children do an amazing job of decorating eggs with nothing more than crayons.

Hunt around a bit and find out where you can get the best buy on eggs. The children will want to do at least two each, and a few extras are essential. Eggs do occasionally crack in boiling, and somebody is certain to smash one of his. For dyeing parties, remember that small-sized, grade B eggs are a good buy. Some stores sell these in lots of two or three dozen at very low cost.

Decide what the children will use for carrying home their treasures. Small paper or plastic bags are often the best choice. Be sure you have enough of these in the house.

When you have your party plans complete, spend a few minutes making a check list of supplies you will need. The one below is offered as a guide. The slight amount of time this takes will be more than repaid when you discover that there is not one single thing you have to rush after at the last minute.

*Materials for Egg-dyeing Party*

Hardcooked, white eggs (at least two for each child)
Egg dye, preferably for use in cold water

168

Cups or other containers for each color of dye

Egg holders or tablespoons, one for each child

Vinegar

Old newspapers

Wax crayons, if you plan to decorate or mark the dyed eggs

Assorted egg decorations, if desired

Small paper or plastic bags for taking the finished eggs home

When the invitations go out, be sure to say that it is to be an egg-dyeing party. Otherwise, you'll have a guest or two appear in his Sunday clothes instead of old jeans and one of his father's cast-off shirts. Remind the children to bring aprons or smocks, if you think jeans won't be enough protection.

The day before the party or early in the morning of that day, hardcook the eggs. Refrigerate them and keep them under refrigeration until about an hour before party time. For easy handling, the eggs should be at room temperature when they are dyed. Prepare the dye and arrange it at intervals around the table before the children come.

When the guests arrive, distribute the eggs and turn them loose. They won't need instructions on what to do if they're over five years old.

Younger children will find dyeing the eggs, a game or two, and plain refreshments party enough. Older ones might want to play more elaborate games, have an egg-decorating contest, or possibly combine the party with an egg hunt. If they decide to have an egg hunt, have each child initial his own eggs so that they can be reclaimed later. An adult should hide the eggs in one area while the children are kept busy somewhere else.

Now that wasn't so bad, was it?

# EGG-DYEING PARTY FOR KINDERGARTNERS

With a bit of advance preparation, an egg-dyeing party for the kindergarten or nursery school set can be great fun for everyone concerned.

About a week ahead of time, send a note to each mother explaining that an egg-dyeing party will be held on a certain date. Ask that the children wear old clothes, and, if it is a school party, have each one bring two hardcooked eggs from home. Enlist the help of other adults for the day.

Collect a supply of empty one-pound cottage cheese containers, check on the vinegar, and buy one package of cold-water egg dye, containing at least four colors. Unless you have a very large number of children, you won't need more. Be sure you have either a spoon or an egg holder for each color dye. And begin to collect old newspapers. As with any other egg-dyeing party, you'll need a great many. It is a wise idea to have a few extra hardcooked eggs on hand, to allow for the inevitable catastrophe.

On the day of the party, cover the tables with a thick layer of newspapers and put another one on the floor under and around the tables. Put a few paper towels on each table for drying the dyed eggs. Prepare the containers of egg dye, and put no more than two on each table. If it is at all possible, just have one color (or one container) of dye on each table. Put out a spoon or an egg holder for each container of dye.

When everything is ready, pencil the owner's initials on the eggs. Then allow the children, one at a time, to dye their eggs. Show them how to dip the egg in and out of the dye solution until they get the desired shade. Dry the eggs on the paper towels.

In addition to the dyed eggs, you might let the children try eggs with simple decorations (see page 53), comic-strip eggs (see page 133), or egg pigs (see page 129).

These activities, topped off with light refreshments, make for a lovely party.

# EASTER EGG HUNTS

As with egg-dyeing parties, the amount of advance planning given to an egg hunt has a good deal to do with the success of the outcome; a well-planned hunt can mean a great deal of fun for the children, no tears, and no property damage, while a badly organized one may end in pure chaos.

## *Where to Hold the Egg Hunt*

If you live in a city apartment, there is really no choice: The egg hunt has to be held indoors. Should you be fortunate enough to have a house in the suburbs or out in the country, hold the hunt outside if at all possible. Since the weather at Easter is unpredictable in most of the United States, have an alternate indoor location ready in case a sudden storm forces you to change your plans.

For an indoor hunt, choose the most childproof—or childproofable—room available and remove all breakable objects which are not actually nailed down; an excited child is not going to worry about the value of a lamp he knocks over. A basement or family room is ideal. But do limit the hunt to one or, at most, two rooms.

If you are considering an egg hunt for a large group of children, investigate the possibility of renting space in a community center or using the recreation room in an apartment house, if some of the participants live there. Or, ask about reserving an area in a nearby park. Charges for the use of these facilities are usually low, but reservations must be made quite far in advance.

# Easter Eggs For Everyone

## *Preparing for the Hunt*

Decide well ahead of time how many prizes you will have. This will depend largely on the ages of the children taking part. With very small, or even primary-age, youngsters, it is a good idea to have a prize for everyone. Older children do not need as many prizes, but do allow for an ample number. Prizes are just as welcome when they are simple; often a candy egg will do very well. If you are planning a hunt for a large group of children, you will probably want to have both large and small prizes. Easter baskets make very good major prizes. Unless you live in a rural area and have the consent of the child's parents, resist the temptation to use live bunnies or baby chicks as awards.

If you like, wrapped pieces of candy may be hidden along with the eggs. This increases the fun and reduces the number of eggs needed. Many people also hide special eggs along with the others. These may be painted gold or silver or may be eggs with the word "prize" marked on them. The finder of one of these eggs gets a special award.

Each participant will need a container of some sort for the eggs he finds. These are provided by the person giving the hunt. They may be made in advance by the child host or hostess, or they can be made on the spot as an activity to keep the guests busy while the eggs are being hidden by adults. Whether the containers are simple or ornate, they should be large enough to hold the eggs and quite sturdy; remember, they have to last through an often-hectic hunt and until the child arrives at home. Plastic bags designed for food storage will do nicely, if nothing else is available.

If containers are to be made at the hunt, provide a supply of *strong* small boxes, flexible wire for handles, materials for decoration, crepe paper strips, and white glue. Decorate the boxes as desired, wrap the handles with crepe paper strips, and attach them to the boxes with heavy wire staples. Or, punch holes near the top edges of the boxes, thread the handles through, and twist them together to fasten in place.

The day before the hunt, dye the eggs and store under refrigeration until it is time to hide them. Prepare any special or golden eggs. Wrap the candy and prizes.

## The Big Day

Try to have the eggs hidden by adults shortly before the guests arrive. Keep the young host or hostess busy somewhere else while the eggs are being hidden. Or, hide the eggs while the children make their containers. Care should be taken that the eggs are neither too hard nor too easy to find. Do not hide eggs too high above the children's heads or too deep in shrubbery.

In a group of children of varying ages and abilities, it is a good idea to handicap the older and abler participants. For example, senior children would have to find two eggs before they could begin to count subsequent eggs toward a prize, the middle-aged children one egg, and the little ones begin counting with the first egg they find. It works out more evenly in the end. The older children have more eggs to carry home and the youngest ones are still in the running for the prizes.

If you decide to combine an egg-dyeing party with an egg hunt, be sure to have the children initial their eggs before they are hidden. They will want to take home their own creations, and initials will forestall possible arguments over ownership.

After the hunt is over, provide refreshments as you would for any other party for children.

## COMMUNITY-WIDE EASTER EGG HUNTS

Many service clubs or troops of older Scouts make community-wide Easter egg hunts an annual project. Hunts for large groups of children are no harder to plan than those for just a few participants. They may actually be easier to conduct because there are so many people available to help with the work.

For an egg hunt for from 250-500 children, begin making plans at least two weeks in advance. Assign a committee to handle the details. If the group already has a committee on child welfare or children's activities, it is a natural task for them.

First, set the date. In many areas, the Saturday before Holy Week is traditionally set aside for the egg hunt. Families planning trips during the school recess have usually not yet left, and children are full of excitement about the approaching holiday. Arrange for the use of a large athletic field or part of a park. If you agree to clean up the facility after the hunt is over, it may be possible to get it without cost.

With a group of this size, it is best to divide the children into five different age groups: toddlers, 2- and 3-year-olds; preschool, 4- and 5-year-olds; first and second grade, 6- and 7-year-olds; third and fourth grades, 8- and 9-year-olds and fifth and sixth grades, 10- to 12-year-olds. Unless mentally retarded children are participating, the top age limit should be 12 regardless of the grade in school.

Purchase from 90-100 dozen eggs from a wholesale dealer and divide them among group members who volunteer to take them home for cooking and dyeing. Or, if you have the equipment to handle quantity cookery, you might prefer to do this at your meeting place. To dye eggs in large lots, put the uncooked eggs in pots and cover them with cold water. Dissolve egg dye in baby food jars using at least 6 times the usual amount of one color to each jar of water. Add a container of dye to each pot of eggs and hardcook as usual (see page 42). When the eggs are cooked, drain off the water and refrigerate the eggs until time to hide them for the hunt.

Early on the morning of the hunt, divide the field into areas according to the age level of the children. Have adults hide the eggs in each area. The ages of the children who will be hunting there should be considered when the eggs are hidden. Hide 2 golden eggs in each section. Add any other extras you like.

Ten-thirty in the morning is a good starting time for the hunt. Have plenty of group members on hand to supervise the children. If appropriate, ask the mayor or other community official to be present to give out the prizes.

For each age group, there are special awards for the children finding the golden eggs. Another prize goes to the child finding the most eggs, and still another may go to that member of the largest participating family who finds the most eggs. For a group of this size, allow approximately 18 prizes in all. Easter baskets filled with candy are good choices for a community-wide egg hunt. Or, if the hunt takes place in a rural area and the parents approve, live Easter bunnies make nice prizes for the children finding the most eggs.

And be sure to notify your local newspaper that the egg hunt will be taking place. Events like this make good human interest stories.

175

# EASTER EGG GAMES

## GERMAN EGG GAME

This game is sometimes known as "Easter Game." It is considered good fun by middle-aged children (7 to 11).[1]

*Number of Players*

Any even number.

*Equipment*

Colored eggs
Cotton or shavings
2 baskets

*Directions*

This game is most interesting when played by only 2 at a time, letting the others watch until their turn comes. Two baskets, some cotton or shavings, and several pretty colored eggs are needed. One basket is shallow and filled with the shavings. The other contains the eggs. One play-

---

[1] From Sarah Ethridge Hunt, *Games and Sports the World Around*, Third Edition, copyright © 1964, The Ronald Press, New York, p. 131.

er is chosen to be the runner while the other tends the baskets. The runner rushes from the starting place to a marked spot and back; during that time the other player tries to transfer the eggs (one by one) from the egg basket to the shallow one. The children then change places and play again. The score depends on the number of eggs transferred. The eggs may be given to the player having the best record.

## EGG GAME

This is another interesting egg game which is best for middle-aged children (7 to 11) . [1]

### Number of Players

From 4 to 10

### Equipment

Cane or rod
6 colored eggs. 1 each: blue, black, red, green, white, and gold.
Large handkerchief

### Directions

This game may be played either indoors or outdoors. When it is played outdoors, the eggs may be set up in sand; indoors they may be propped up in cotton. Each player takes a turn being blindfolded and trying to touch the different eggs with a rod or cane while the

---

[1] From Hunt, *Games and Sports the World Around,* copyright © 1964, The Ronald Press, New York, p. 184.

others sing the rhyme below. The score of each player is based on his accuracy in executing the actions suggested in the song.

*Mike and Meg, Pat and Peg,*
*Watch me tap this Easter egg:*
*Blue and black, green, red, and white*
*Value at two, four, six, five, and one:*
*Should I tap the egg of gold,*
*That should be mine to hold.*

The player who first scores 20 wins the game.

## EGG-SACKLY WHAT

This game requires a bit of advance preparation, but it is a tantalizer. Clever mothers will find a use for it at other than party time, too. The players may be of almost any age, but the game has the most appeal to middle-aged children (7 to 11).

### Number of Players

Any number.

### Equipment

Blown eggs
An assortment of small objects—beans, dried peas, rice, small pebbles, paper clips, buttons, or anything else that will fit inside the eggshells and rattle
Opaque tape
Pencil and paper for each player

*Directions*

Slightly enlarge the hole in one end of each blown egg. Carefully fill the shell with enough rice, beans, etc., so that the egg will rattle when it is shaken. Use only one kind of object in each egg. Pencil a number on each egg, and keep a record of what goes into each one. Cover the hole with a piece of opaque tape. Prepare about 6 eggs this way.

Each player shakes each egg, and then writes down the number of the egg and what he thinks is inside it. When all players have had a turn, take off the tape and turn the contents onto the table. The player with the most correct guesses wins.

## DANISH EGG ROLLING

This is the Danish version of the ever-popular egg rolling which appeals to middle-aged children (7 to 11).

*Number of Players*

Any even number—keep the ages similar in the first rounds.

*Equipment*

Hardcooked eggs, dyed

*Directions*

Set up a course with a starting line and a finishing line. Outdoors, a lawn would be ideal for this; indoors, a gymnasium or other place where the eggs can be rolled for some distance is best.

## Easter Eggs For Everyone

Two children stand, side-by-side at the starting point, egg in hand. On signal, both start down the course, walking or running and rolling their eggs ahead of them. The child who is able to roll his egg for the greatest distance without cracking the shell wins the round. If an uncracked egg stops before the player crosses the finish line, he may pick it up and roll again. Repeat with other children. When all of the children have had a turn on the course, have winners roll against winners. Keep on until only one child remains.

## EIERTIKKEN

In the Netherlands, as in most of Europe, Easter Monday is a holiday. On that day, the Dutch people pack dyed, hard-boiled eggs in baskets and take them to out-of-door spots where the eggs are used in contests. These contests are called *Eiertikken*. These contests appeal to all ages.

### Number of Players

Any even number—but keep ages similar during the first rounds.

### Equipment

Hardcooked eggs, dyed, at least 2 of each color

### Directions

The players form 2 lines which stand, facing each other. Each contestant holds his egg in his hand and stands opposite the player on the other team whose egg is the same color as his own.

On signal, each player tries to crack the shell of his opponent's egg by striking it with his own. The winner keeps his adversary's egg.

The contest is repeated, with winners pitted against winners, until only one player remains. The player with the most eggs is declared the local Eiertikken champion.

## EGG RACE

This is a good game for middle-aged children to play at an Easter party. It is best suited to children 7 to 11 years old. It does not require complicated equipment and can be played indoors very successfully.

### Number of Players

From 8 to 24

### Equipment

4 sheets of cardboard. The cardboard from newly laundered shirts will do very well.
4 blown eggs, decorated if desired
Prize. This does not have to be elaborate.

### Directions

Set up a starting line on one side of the room and a finish line on the other side of the room.

Divide the players into groups of 4. Place the eggs

181

along the starting line. Give each player a sheet of card-board.

Explain that the players are to fan the hollow eggs across the room and over the finish line, using the card-board to fan the eggs. This sounds much easier than it actually is, since the eggs are not round. The first player to get his egg over the finish line wins that heat.

Repeat with the other groups of players. Then play the winners against each other. The winner of the final heat gets a prize.

## EASTER EGG ROLL

This is a good rough and tumble variation for the tradition-al egg rolling. It is best for children, 7 to 11, not wearing their good clothes.

### Number of Players

From 2 to 6

### Equipment
Hardcooked eggs

### Directions

Set up a course with a starting line and a finishing line. Provide each child with a hardboiled egg. The players put their eggs on the floor on the starting line. On signal, they begin pushing the egg to the finishing line using only their noses. The first one to reach the finishing line wins.

182

# WHITHER EGGSHELL?

This is a variation on the egg race, perhaps a bit more sophisticated than some versions. It is best for older elementary or junior high school children, aged 10 to 14.

## Number of Players

Ideally, from 2 to 6

## Equipment

Blown eggs with the shells reinforced. One for each player.

## Directions

Reinforce blown eggshells by covering the holes with gummed cloth or strong gummed paper cut into a ¼-inch circle. Barring any accidents, this will make the shells strong enough to be used quite a few times.

Lay out a course, either indoors or outdoors, having a plainly marked starting line and a finishing line 30 or 40 feet away. Place an eggshell for each player on the starting line. To give enough room for movement, the shells should be 3 feet apart.

On signal, each player kneels behind his eggshell. At the command, "Go," he tries to blow his eggshell across the finish line. He must obey these rules:

1-The player must stay on his hands and knees.

2-The egg must be moved only by blowing.

3-The egg must not be blown so hard that it rolls end over end.

4-Any player who breaks one of these rules is given a

penalty of 10 feet. He must move his egg back and continue the race.

The first player to get his eggshell across the finish line while obeying the rules of the game is the winner.

## WHITHER EGGSHELL VARIATION

The game may be played with partners facing each other, one at the starting line, the other at the finishing line. One partner blows the egg to the finish line. The other partner takes over there and blows the egg back to the starting line. The first pair to complete the course are the winners.

## EIERLESEN

*Eierlesen*, or egg-gathering, is a somewhat sophisticated form of egg-rolling. Very popular in Germany, it requires considerable skill and has much appeal to older children or adults who find the traditional egg rolling too childish for their tastes. In the Black Forest region, *Eierlesen* is often done from the backs of horses or while the players ride bicycles.

### Number of Players

Any number—but participation is best limited to children over the age of 10. Eierlesen can get rough.

### Equipment Needed

Space for a racing track
Hardcooked eggs, dyed
Baskets or other containers for the eggs

184

Easter Egg Games

*Directions*

Using the lanes of a racing track, or, marking out your own lanes on a long, flat course, place dyed eggs at intervals extending for some distance. Decide on a time limit for gathering the eggs.

On signal, the players start down the track, each in his own lane, gathering eggs as they run. The winner is the player who gathers the most eggs in the specified time, or who crosses the finish line first with the most eggs.

## EGG RUNNING CONTEST

This novel relay requires real control. If you want to be daring, use uncooked! eggs instead of hardcooked ones. This is best for children 10 and up.

*Number of Players*

Any even number.

*Equipment Needed*

Teaspoon for each player
2 eggs, usually hardcooked

*Directions*

Set up starting and finishing lines. Divide the players into 2 teams for a relay race. Give each player a teaspoon with instructions to hold it by the handle between his teeth. Place an egg in the bowl of the spoon held by the first player in each team. On signal, the team members walk to the finishing line and back keeping their hands clasped behind their backs and without dropping the egg. Each team member takes his turn until every player has successfully run the race. The team finishing first is declared the winner.

# bibliography

Aikman, Lonnelle. *The Living White House.* Washington, D. C.: White House Historical Association, 1966.

Almedingen, Martha E. *My St. Petersburg.* New York: W. W. Norton & Co., 1970.

Bale, R. O. *Creative Nature Crafts.* Minneapolis: Burgess Publishing Co., 1959.

Brown, Audrey. "Fabulous New Notions in Easter Eggs." *Family Circle,* 74 (April, 1969).

Carter, Joan L. "The Egg and Dye." *The American Girl,* 35 (April, 1952).

Crocker, Betty. *Betty Crocker's Hostess Cookbook.* New York: Western Publishing Co., 1967.

Freeman, Louis M. *Betty Crocker's Parties for Children.* New York: Western Publishing Co., 1964.

Gaer, Joseph. *Holidays Around the World.* Boston: Little, Brown, 1953.

Harbin, E. O. *Games for Boys and Girls.* New York: Abingdon Press, 1951.

Hawley, Henry. *Fabergé and His Contemporaries.* Cleveland, Ohio: Western Reserve University Press, 1967.

Herder, K. G. *Painted Easter Eggs.* New York: Herder Book Center, 1968.

Hunt, Sarah E. *Games and Sports the World Around,* 3rd ed. New York: Ronald Press, 1964.

Kay, Helen. *An Egg Is for Wishing.* New York: Abelard-Schuman, 1966.

Leach, Maria, ed. *Funk and Wagnalls Standard Dictionary of Folklore, Mythology, and Legend,* vol. 1. New York: Funk and Wagnalls, 1949.

Leeming, Joseph. *Holiday Craft and Fun*. Philadelphia: J. B. Lippincott Co., 1950.

Lord, Priscilla and Foley, Daniel J. *Easter the World Over*. Philadelphia: Chilton Books, 1971.

Papashvily, Helen, and Papashvily, George. *Russian Cooking*. Foods of the World. New York: Time-Life Books, 1970.

Parrott, Lora Lee. *Encyclopedia of Party Ideas for Children*. Grand Rapids: Zondervan Publishing House, 1966.

Purdy, Susan. *Festivals for You to Celebrate*. Philadelphia: J. B. Lippincott Co., 1969.

Schegger, Theresia M. *Make Your Own Mobiles*. Translated by Paul Kuttner. New York: Sterling Publishing Co., 1965.

Sechrist, Elizabeth, and Woolsey, Janette. *It's Time for Easter*. Philadelphia: Macrae Smith, 1961.

Sechrist, Elizabeth. *Red Letter Days*, rev. ed. Philadelphia: Macrae Smith Co., 1965.

Spicer, Dorothy G. *Festivals of Western Europe*. New York: H. W. Wilson Co., 1958.

Surmach, Yaroslava. "Ukrainian Easter Eggs." New York: Surma Book and Music Co., 1957. (Pamphlet)

Walther, Willard. *Hobbycraft for Juniors*. New York: Lantern Press, 1967.

Weiser, Frances X. *Handbook of Christian Feasts and Customs*. New York: Harcourt Brace Jovanovich, 1958.

# index

189

# Index

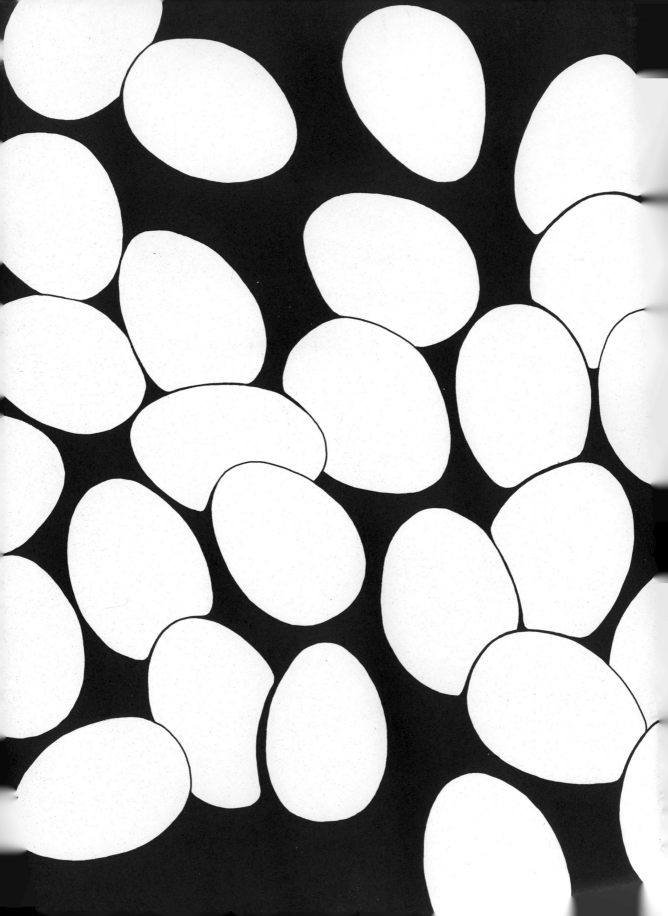